CONVERSATIONS
ON Success

Hugs and Smiles,

Joean

Interior formatting and design: Brittany Stewart
Cover Graphic Design: Emmy Shubert
Editor: Sandra Pinkoski

Insight Publishing Company
647 Wall Street
Sevierville, Tennessee 37862

10 9 8 7 6 5 4 3 2

Printed in the United States.

ISBN-10: 1-60013-208-1
ISBN-13: 978-1-60013-208-7

Table of Contents

A Message from the Publisher... vii

Chapter 1   Robert Paisola 1

Chapter 2   Tom Hopkins 11

Chapter 3   Joeann Fossland 25

Chapter 4   Sue Becker 37

Chapter 5   Duane Cashin 47

Chapter 6   John Gray 59

Chapter 7   Chuck McCants 73

Chapter 8   Bruce Carter 87

Chapter 9   David Hira 101

Chapter 10   Daved Beck 113

Chapter 11   Danny Cox 123

A Message from the Publisher

Some of my most rewarding experiences in business, and for that matter in my personal life, have been at meetings, conventions, or gatherings after the formal events have concluded. Inevitably, small groups of ten to fifteen men and women gather together to rehash the happenings of the day and to exchange war stories, recently heard jokes, or the latest gossip from their industry. It is in these informal gatherings where some of the best lessons can be learned.

Usually, in informal groups of professionals, there are those who clearly have lived through more battles and learned more lessons than the others. These are the men and women who are really getting the job done and everyone around the room knows it. When they comment on the topic of the moment, they don't just spout the latest hot theory or trend, and they don't ramble on and on without a relevant point. These battle scarred warriors have lessons to share that everyone senses are just a little more real, more relevant, and therefore worthy of more attention.

These are the kind of people we have recruited to offer their insights and expertise for *Conversations On Success*. The book is filled with frank and powerful discussions with men and women who are making a significant impact on their culture, in their field, and on their colleagues and clients. It is ripe with "the good stuff," as an old friend of mine used to always say. Inside these pages you'll find ideas, insights, strategies, and philosophies that are working with real people, in real companies, and under real circumstances.

It is our hope that you keep this book with you until you've dog-eared every chapter and made so many notes in the margins that you have trouble seeing the original words on the pages. There is treasure here. Enjoy digging!

Interviews conducted by:

David E. Wright
President, International Speakers Network

Chapter One

An interview with . . .

Robert Paisola

David Wright (Wright)

Today we're talking with Robert Paisola. Robert is a dynamic and energetic speaker, riveting his audiences' attention throughout his presentations to the very last sentence. Each and every presentation he makes provides a unique blend of motivation and education. His listeners and readers around the world receive practical techniques that can be used immediately.

He sees and seeks to fulfill the need for communication, education, and positive influence in our rapidly changing society. Robert Paisola understands the need to constantly customize all of his publications and seminars for a rapidly changing world economy. As a leader, Robert Paisola's philosophy is simply, "Don't count what you have, but what you have been given—and that is the true meaning of success."

Robert, why do you feel that you are successful?

Robert Paisola (Paisola)

One of the biggest reasons I believe I am successful is that I believe in the power of delegation. Every single person with whom I have a working relationship knows what he or she is supposed to do—and each one of them does it. I give people responsibility and I let them make decisions.

Secondly, I continue to educate myself. I educate myself through regular education as well as secondary education, personal empowerment, and growth seminars. I also read and I am constantly networking with the people I meet.

Third, I take action. I am a goal-setter. I set goals that are measurable, specific, and attainable. They are goals I know I can attain. That is the way my mind works. I am completely focused twenty-four hours a day on achievement of those goals.

Wright

Once you delegate it what kind of management do you do? Do you stay out of the way or do you micromanage?

Paisola

I am a firm believer in giving people the ability to do their jobs. I give somebody an assignment and responsibility and he or she has the ability to succeed or to fail on his or her own. We hire the best and we expect the best from those people.

As a manager it gives me great pleasure to say that very seldom do we have people who simply don't "get it." I simply pass it along, I delegate it, and it gets done. It is a great philosophy and a great way to do business.

I can tell you right now where I will be in a month and where I will be in a year from now; and that is a very powerful way to manage.

Wright

What has been your biggest obstacle or fear? How do you deal with setbacks and fears?

Paisola

That is a good question. The biggest obstacle for me is fear itself. It took me over nine months to overcome fear before I was able to do my first deal, before I was able to put myself in the public eye, and before I was able to go out and grow my organization. I knew inside that I had that ability to create an enterprise, to create a foundation, to create financial abundance for my family. I learned to get over the fear of actually doing it. The way to get through fear is simply to accept it and move through it.

With the continuing education philosophy, I was able to experience different types of training. I was given the ability to move through the fear that we all face at some point in our lives. Once I went through the fear I was able to simply know that no matter what I went after I would be able to obtain.

Wright

What do you believe is going to happen to the world economy in the next ten years?

Paisola

There is no question that we are headed for a complete devaluation of the Real Estate markets around the nation. We are looking at some of the biggest areas in the country that are going to go through complete financial turmoil.

We believe that oil is going to cost $100 a barrel. That is simply a supply-and-demand issue. For some people it's going to be the worst time. For smart investors—people with whom we work—it can possibly be the best time. The people who are going to be hurt are those with investment properties for which they really think there is no down side.

We are concentrating, as an organization, on three different areas: the California area, Texas, and the Florida markets. Those areas have been hit hard. People who are in those areas have to have a solution to these critical issues because some of those houses are $200,000 to $300,000 upside down—they have that much negative equity. We are seeing companies as large as Countrywide look at bankruptcy as a serious option because of their exposure in these markets.

It is extremely important that borrowers are able to go out, find people who can assist them, and then create a mutual win-win so they can stay in their houses or walk away from their house with their head held high, as opposed to an eminent foreclosure action.

Wright

So there are people just walking away from their houses?

Paisola

Yes, we are seeing it every day. We get lists here at our company, Western Capital (www.MyCollector.com), that show us all of the "Real Estate Owned Properties" (REOs) by state. These are all the properties repossessed by the banks around the country. Just today, we received five hundred of those from the southern and northern California markets alone. You can also imagine what we receive from Florida and Texas. People simply cannot take that kind of financial hit.

A lot of what is happening now was preceded by events that happened four or five years ago when national lenders started issuing "Interest Only Loans." They started giving the consumer the ability to simply pay the minimum interest amount on a real estate loan, and then guess what? It got more expensive as the interest rate increased. That is why we believe 2008 and 2009 are going to be an extremely volatile period for Real Estate owners throughout the country.

Wright

What do you believe that it is going to take to be financially secure in the coming years?

Paisola

The bottom line is that you must be financially literate—take advice from people who have gone through what you are going through and take advice from the experts. Take advice from people who have seen it and have done it. Some of them have succeeded, but all of them have rebounded. Some, like Donald Trump, have failed, only to have grown bigger beyond their wildest expectations. Most Real Estate brokers and stock brokers are not rich; that's what's interesting to us, yet people take their financial advice. Most schools teach you how to go out and get a job, but are they rich. Do they teach you how to go out and become financially successful and truly financially abundant? No.

It's that constant educational process that brings people to the next level. People have to constantly realize that educating themselves about finance is going to absolutely affect their financial security in the coming years.

Wright

What methods do you use to keep yourself focused on your goals and desires?

Paisola

This is a tough question for me because I get emotional about this. For so long I had a problem in not believing in myself. I didn't believe I had the ability to do what it takes to be continually successful until I learned about the power of "Visualization."

The power of visualization goes along with "if you can perceive it, you will achieve it." I use this in my everyday life. The power of visualization allows me to see my life as I want it to be in all areas in the current tense. In other words, Visualization allows me to see myself exactly as I want to be, as though I'm watching a movie of my life in the present tense and just waiting for time to catch up. That is how I am completely focused on my goals and desires.

Wright

Rob, we have read many of your writings in magazines and books around the nation, and in one of your articles you wrote, "The quality of a person's life is in direct proportion to the quality of their peer group." Can you explain this?

Paisola

You are what you eat! If you choose to be successful and you are willing to do whatever it takes to get there, then you must be willing to sacrifice to climb the mountains that so very few people want to go and explore. The only way to do this is with a guide. To be able to become successful, it is absolutely essential to have a mentor, to have a leader, to have somebody who has been there before you.

In business, if I want to become successful, I want to be around people like a Donald Trump, Anthony Robbins, and Colin Powell—people who have been through the mud, only to have bounced back. Why? So that I don't have to experience those same pitfalls that they've gone through.

I ask people at our seminars, "How many of you have ever failed to achieve something significant in your life?" Everybody's hand goes up. Why is that? Because we have all achieved success and we have all experienced failure. It doesn't matter who it is.

Taking those failures and moving forward with them makes you a true success. The only failure is simply lying down and saying, "No, I give up!" Whether you are a Supreme Court justice, whether you're Al Gore or Tony Robbins—no matter who you are—it doesn't matter, you are going to have ups and downs. That is something that we really concentrate on as we look at our dreams and goals.

Wright

Someone told me one day several years ago that if you see a turtle on top of a fence post, you can bet he didn't get up there by himself. Are there any mentors who have really made a difference in your life?

Paisola

The list is long and the list includes many. Anthony Robbins comes to mind, a man named James Smith, R. G. Williams, and Hans Berger, CEO of the Impact Trainings Program. My dad taught me the fundamentals of what it takes to stick it out. The people I deal with on a daily basis as I attend shows at the Learning Annex and the people I meet around the world are also on that list. Some people would consider them celebrities, but I don't look at them as celebrities—I look at them as people who have all gone through ups and downs and have the ability to take their lives to the next level.

As you said, that turtle didn't get there by himself. How many of us try to get it right? How many of us are always trying? And that's all we end up with at the end of the day when we look at our results. You see, trying doesn't get you anywhere. Doing—action—is what creates success. I learned that through one of my mentors, just like the turtle that was able to get on top of the fence—he didn't do it himself, he knew somebody who was going to be able to assist him to get him there.

Wright

What are some of the biggest challenges facing people today?

Paisola

In today's world of "give it to me now," we are granted instant access to almost anything we want with a simple click of the mouse. The Internet has become a revolution. It has changed the way we live. We are able to find out things that happened seconds ago in an instant, 10,000 miles away, by turning on CNN. The days of the traditional newspaper are over. The days of journalism where you have executive committee meetings trying to determine the correct ways to report or not report an event are over. The blog revolution is here. Generation X is creating an absolute whirlwind of people who create that "give it to me now!" mentality.

We see movies that cost hundreds of millions of dollars and we see them and want them now. We don't go into the theater wondering what it took to create that movie. For instance, recently I saw the movie *Transformers*. That movie features some of the most amazing CGI technical effects that have ever been created by mankind and it took the team who created that movie years to do what appeared on the big screen. In just two hours I was able to raise my sense of awareness and I was able to listen and see that amazing technological marvel that was around me. I was literally in the experience.

Another thing I am able to do is to rent a private jet through Net Jets at a moment's notice. I can be halfway across the world in a matter of hours. One other thing that I'm concerned about is that in a world full of choices, we seem to be experiencing less happiness. Why is that? Why is it that when we are given so much—we have the ability to take everything that we want in our lives and self-create it through the power of abundance—yet we are not experiencing sustainable joy? That is a great question to think about.

Wright

I recently saw a television news program where you said, "It is not the events of our lives that shape us, but our beliefs as to what those events mean." What do you mean by this?

Paisola

One thing we know as human beings is that life is not always a bed of roses. We have been preconditioned to react to certain situations in either a positive or negative way, depending upon the situation. In general, we've been taught how to react when something happens.

One thing that has made me successful is that I truly believe everything in our lives that happens to us or around us happens for a reason. There are no accidents. Because there are no accidents, this means the good things that happen, along with the bad things, are there to make us grow. These things happen to let us see the difference, to create our own legacy, to be able to create financial abundance, and to be able to pull our head out of the sand sometimes. That's why both negative and positive things happen.

It is so important to understand that we all have the ability to be successful. We have the ability to achieve success through our own beliefs and through our own actions. We do not have to continue to live the lie by acting in that preconditioned way I mentioned earlier. We all have the ability to break the barriers of our history and to move forward. The sky is the limit.

Getting back to the subject of mentors, if you want to be successful, surround yourself with successful people. If you choose not to be successful, that's easy—hang out with people who don't have any money, don't have any stamina or ambition, hang out with people who don't have any willpower, and who don't believe they have the ability to make it. Then you will see what you will become because you will become direct fruit of the trees you hang around.

Wright

What advice would you give to young people who see their lives as a dead end? This includes individuals who are classified as convicted felons.

Paisola

Thank you for that question because this is one of the most powerful and absolute goals I have as an international speaker and author.

Tear down the walls of the revolving door of our prison systems. So many people believe that just because their parents went to prison, they are going to have to go to prison. Just because their mothers and fathers didn't have financial success, they are not going to have financial success. To every single person reading this—no matter where you are from, no matter where you have been— *you have the ability to create your own destiny.*

The first thing I would say is that you are not your history and you truly have the power within you to make a difference in the world. I'm not talking about the world in your community—I'm talking about the world in general. Things have happened in my life that, at the time, seemed absolutely tragic, but see what I'm doing now—I'm co-authoring this book with Dr. John Grey, author of *Men are from Mars, Women are from Venus.*

Another book deal that I just signed last week is a book titled *Blueprint for Success.* I am co-authoring this book with the wonderful Dr. Stephen R. Covey.

I created that. I chose success. In today's society, it is so easy to sit back and point the finger of blame at others, while not accepting accountability for our actions, thereby giving ourselves an easy out. It is so simple to sit back in your chair and look at the world saying, "Wow, this group of people does not deserve to move forward in life." Every single thing in your life that happens, happens for a reason. It is not what happens to you, but it is what you do with that experience by helping others people within your sphere of influence that gives you the inner feeling that you can and will truly make a difference.

When I watch the news, I do not see a lot of positive news any more. As a media guest, I am contacted daily by producers wanting my opinion on very controversial subjects. Rarely do I ever receive a call asking me, "Robert, how do you feel about that nineteen-year-old mayor of Mercer, Pennsylvania, who chose to become the youngest mayor in the nation—and did it!" The media loves to talk about the negative things in the world. I did a two-hour interview with a reporter named Stephen Dark, and when the article was printed everything was negative. There was no discussion about our foundation, no discussion about the people we have helped—nothing positive! What does that say about us as a society?

When you bring something positive to the table and you talk about offender reform or decreasing mandatory minimum sentences they don't want to hear it. That is why I created a foundation called www.Prisonpartners.com. This organization was created to let people know that they too have the ability—no matter what their background, no matter what the history, no matter what's happened to them—to become successful.

I know a lot of people who are reading this have had experience with sexual abuse. I also know that you have lived with that your entire life. The good news is that you can overcome it. The good news is you have the ability to move past the things that happened to you when you were younger. You do not have to be held victim—to be held hostage—to that abuse any longer. That is also what I'm passionate about.

No matter where you've been, you too can co-author a book with a renowned author. You too can go out and create your own destiny. Guess what it takes? It takes your making the first move! Nobody is going to walk up to you and ask, "Would you like to co-author a book?" Would you like to have success in your life? Would you like to experience financial abundance in your life? You have to grab the bull by the horns and go for it!

My friend, whenever you make the decision to truly "go for it," you will achieve the most amazing results that you've ever achieved in your life!

To convey this fact to people is truly my passion and mission in life.

Wright

That's a powerful message.

Paisola

Thank you, Mr. Wright.

About the Author

Robert Paisola is driven by a passion for people and motivating them to reach for the highest standards of success. As founder and president of many international corporations including Western Capital and The Success Training Network, Robert trains sales and marketing professionals who want to strive to get to the top—and stay there. He is a nationally recognized criminal rights activist and is very involved with assisting inmates and their families who have been abused by the justice system. His innovative, no-nonsense approach is based on applying what he has observed in his fifteen-plus years in sales, motivational speaking, and debt collection training, thus revealing the common business habits of the top 20 percent of sales performers in all organizations. While in Mexico, he uncovered a large time share "fractional sales" scam at the Playa Del Sol Grand Hotel.

Robert's approach works; that's why New York-based *Success Magazine* has rated Robert Paisola as one of the top five most effective sales-training professionals in the market today. His newest book was just released and is available on Amazon.com. He is also a noted speaker on the topics of Group Dynamics, Change Management, Investing, Real Estate, Asset Protection, and Stock Investments. Routinely distinguished by The National Speakers Forum, Robert is also a regular contributor to *BusinessWeek* magazine, CNN, CNNFN, XM Satellite Radio, *The Wall Street Journal,* Telemundo International, National Public Radio, and many other organizations. Robert is also an international travel writer and Certified Expert for magazines such as Conde Nast Publications and The National Geographic Society. His award-winning investigative reporting articles have gained him worldwide recognition. He continues to look deep into the world of his seventy-eight-year-old nemesis Bill Bauer a.k.a. CreditWrench or Billie (Bill) Bauer, in Oklahoma at www.BillBauerFacts.com. If you are looking for personalized service, Robert now has a reduced fee schedule for readers.

Robert Paisola
Western Capital
Phone: 877.517.9555
E-mail: robert@mycollector.com
www.ReputationMD.com
www.WesternCapitalVIP.com
www.RobertPaisola.net
www.RobertPaisola.com

Chapter Two

An *interview with* . . .

Tom Hopkins

David Wright (Wright)

Today we're talking with Tom Hopkins. Tom is a sales legend. Many believe that natural ability is enough to make you successful in a sales career, but the truth of the matter is that natural skill combined with "how to" training is the real secret to high level productivity. Having learned this lesson the hard way, Tom is quick to admit that his early sales career was not successful. After benefiting from professional training, he became a dedicated student, internalizing and refining sales techniques that enabled him to become a sales leader in his industry.

Tom's credibility lies in his track record and the track records of the students he has trained over the years. He has personally trained over three million students on five continents. He has shared the stage with some of the great leaders of our times including Ret. General Norman Schwarzkopf, former President George Bush and Barbara Bush, Secretary of State Colin Powell, and Lady Margaret Thatcher.

Tom has authored twelve books, including *How to Master the Art of Selling* and *Selling For Dummies*™. His first book, *How to Master the Art of Selling*, has sold over 1.6 million copies and has been translated into ten languages. It is required reading for new salespeople by sales and management professionals in a wide variety of industries.

Tom was a pioneer in bringing broadcast-quality video training to the marketplace. Over 16,000 video sales training systems are utilized in-house by companies around the world. His audio cassette programs have long been lauded for their quality, comprehensiveness, along with his workbooks with word-for-word phraseology.

Through the ups and downs of a seller, a career as a business owner, professional speaker, and trainer, Tom Hopkins has maintained his dedication to the continued growth of his students. He firmly believes that everyone can benefit from utilizing his proven techniques, ideas, concepts, and values.

Tom, welcome to *Conversations on Success*.

Tom Hopkins (Hopkins)

Well, thank you, David! And it's so nice after all these years to have a chance to visit with you.

Wright

Tom, after reading an article you wrote titled "Making Connections," it occurred to me that people coming into sales think that networking is only for high-level businesspeople. Can you explain what networking is and how new salespeople can take advantage of it?

Hopkins

First of all, when people use networking, they are taking advantage of a basic law—the Law of Reciprocity. That law basically says, "If I do something good for you, you will feel similarly obligated to do something good for me." That's what networking really is. It's getting together with groups of people who are not in your same industry—so there is no competition involved—then sharing possible leads.

For example, if you just think about it, every three years almost 95 percent of the American population will buy a new car. Every four to five years about 90 percent will buy a new home. And everyone should have help in insurance and financial services to prepare for their golden years. So if you only look at those three industries as examples, you can find people to network with.

When I first learned of this concept I decided to find the top automobile dealership salesperson, the top insurance salesperson, and I was of course in real estate. IBM had just started to blossom, so I got the number one IBM rep I could find in the area. I called them all, and found the top person in each company. We met and decided that we were going to try to find out if we could send leads to each other. And that is how my experience in "networking" began!

Today most companies ask their people to join organizations like their local Chamber of Commerce—to go wherever there's a meeting of people—and try to exchange business cards and see if they can't find a few people to build a networking opportunity with.

Many years ago it wasn't called networking, but that's what people call it today. Networking is taking advantage of what other people have to offer and they, in turn, take advantage of what you have to offer. That way you both grow to reach your goals more rapidly sending leads back and forth and having a network group.

The field of selling can beat you up—it's emotionally draining. If you have three or four people in a network you meet with who are up-lifting and can talk with you about how well they're doing and get you back on track, that's another great reason for networking!

Wright

In that same article you advocated techniques such as staying in touch, actually asking for help, and volunteering to help as methods of networking. Can you expand on these?

Hopkins

First of all, I think that's the key. I think you need to have a planning meeting in your networking group. Let's say you meet every Tuesday morning at 7:30. You meet and have a cup of coffee and you all talk about how you're doing. You then try to see if you can all bring a lead to the table that one of the folks can go ahead and contact.

Also, networking is in an excellent way a way of saying to yourself, "I'm going to try to help as many other people as I can. I'll volunteer, I might go and join as many community and charitable organizations as I can. I'm going to do my best to help, and thus I'll also network and meet all the folks in that organization."

Wright

Recently I was going through some notes I had written from another of your writings titled *Turning Little Dollars into Big Dollars*. You wrote that, "One of the biggest mistakes salespeople make is to market their product to someone and stop there." Can you explain what you mean?

Hopkins

When people invest in your product or service obviously, by making that commitment, they have said, "I like you, I trust you, and I'm happy to do business with you." But you don't stop there. I think you should send them a thank you note for doing business. You should then set up a process where you do your best to see if they might give you referrals. I've found that most people who really like and trust you at the closing of a sale will afterward be more than happy to say that they know a couple of people who might also be interested. Then you need to follow up and ask if you can help some of those folks. Many people will give you referrals.

Most salespeople make a sale and that's the end of it instead of saying, "I have a philosophy: when I sell a house, my goal is to stay in touch, follow up, and to see if I might be able to make three or four other sales over the years from referrals to people you know who are friends, relatives, and so forth."

Wright

You have said that there is an emotional process that leads to a purchase. If I remember correctly, it involves a new development in the buyer's self-image. Will you tell us what you mean and how salespeople can spot these changes?

Hopkins

I've always believed that over the years with the hundreds and hundreds of houses I've sold (my background being real estate) that I have found that the actual purchasing decision is not logical—it's *emotional*. There is an emotional thing you do with people with the right questions, by asking them certain things that create an emotional build. Too many people think that someone's going to come up with a logical reason to buy a car, a house, insurance, or whatever it is. The truth is that the final decision is made emotionally, and then buyers defend what they did logically with reasons that you as the salesperson give them.

Wright

That does sound like a process that can be learned!

Hopkins

It is. That's what's exciting—all the elements in the art of selling can be learned. And I just want to share this with all the people who might be really paying attention to this. There are two extremes of personality and temperament types: One is the interesting extrovert, and the other is the interested introvert.

The interesting extrovert is the person who's outgoing and gregarious and talkative and charming and witty. Those people gravitate into sales because they are very talkative.

On the other side of the spectrum is the interested introvert. These people are a little timid, a little shy, they don't think they can sell, they're afraid of the process of talking to strangers. The sad truth is that the interested introvert can do *better* in sales long-term than the interesting extrovert because the interested introvert is interested in other people and he or she is willing to listen. Interested introverts are great listeners, they ask questions, and they give up control of conversation. The interesting extrovert has the usual personality you'd expect of salespeople. They're talkative and overbearing, aggressive, and they want to control everything. So if you're an interested introvert, don't be afraid of selling. You can do great!

If you're an interested extrovert, just lighten up a bit and start with more questions than with trying to overtake folks by telling them what they should do.

Wright

Your students have told you that one of their biggest challenges is their clients are not loyal. What advice do you give your students to help them overcome this problem?

Hopkins

This is one thing that has changed in our culture. In fact, people sometimes ask me, "Tom, you've been doing this sales training for thirty years; what has changed?" The main thing that has changed is that people don't have the long-term loyalty with a sales representative that they used to have. There are many reasons for that. Some people who are reading this may be selling a product where the decision-maker works for a company that is just totally concerned with profit—if the decision-maker can save two cents on an item for the entire company, it could mean a lot of money, so they aren't loyal to that salesperson.

The first thing I want to say is to not be upset—that's just the way the culture is. Secondly, here are some ideas to keep clients loyal: Number One, you really have to keep in touch with them and make them realize that they will do better because of what you do. For example, if I sold computers and I had a client company with a very busy managing director or vice president who was in charge of buying computers and computer related items, if I can get some of the responsibility off him I make him look good to the whole company for what I do. As a result he will almost delegate authority to me.

I know some salespeople who don't really sell anymore. They control the company's inventory of a product. Then, of course, the decision-maker is thrilled that he or she doesn't have to worry about it. The salesperson has been given control of the inventory. He or she handles everything and is not really selling. The salesperson controls the company's inventory and earns a nice fee at the end of the year.

Wright

In my business, marketing and booking speakers, getting to speak to the right person who can make a buying decision is sometimes a difficult task. How do you suggest we get through the company "gate-keepers" and speak to the right person?

Hopkins

This is a fun little game you have to play. I hope the people reading this realize that selling or a business activity is like a game—it's a competition. Now, if I were talking to a straight sales commission person who had to market a product or service to earn his or her income, I'd say, "Hey, you have a game that you have to play to get past gate-keepers." The gate-keepers are normally those who answer the phone first, then passes the call to the executive assistant who hides the decision-maker.

Here are some of the keys, David. First, when marketers or salespeople call a company they have to come across with a different way of addressing what they are going to do. For example, I suggest they call and let's say a receptionist answers the phone. If I were doing the calling I would say, "Hi, my name is Tom Hopkins. I'm in business in the community." This creates a rapport—they're in business, I'm in business. Then I'd say, "I really need to talk to the person in your company who is in charge of increasing profits or eliminating overhead. Who might that be?"

The receptionist hears the words "increasing profits" or "eliminating overhead," and she has no idea what this means, but she's thinking this is what the company needs to do, just as all companies today need to do. That one little sentence will motivate her to get me to the decision-maker. Now often they'll say, "Well, that will be Mr. Brown, and I'll put you through to his secretary." Of course, I get Mr. Brown's secretary on the phone and I say, "Hi, my name is Tom Hopkins. I'm in business in the community and I would like to refer people to your company and show Mr. Brown ways that he might eliminate some overhead and increase profits. May I speak with him please?"

Then the secretary may stall and say, "Well, he's not available," or "He's not in," or, "Do you have an appointment?"

I reply, "Let him know I called. Would you please write this down? My name is Tom Hopkins. Make sure he knows that I'm a *local business person*, just like he is, so please, on the message would you please write 'Tom Hopkins, local business person, wanting to refer business to our company'?"

Now I'll guarantee you that when he comes in, he'll get that message and he'll ask "Who is this?"

"Well I'm not sure," the secretary will reply.

And because you didn't leave your phone number (*never* leave your phone number) he'll be curious! Here's a local businessperson who wants to refer business to the company. Remember, this is the game—it's a game you play, but when I use this method I met almost every decision-maker. Why? It was because when I called back the person will ask, "What do you mean you're going to refer business back to us?"

I'll say, "You know what? You have the largest Mercedes dealership in the city. I'm going to be working with people who want a Mercedes in the future—can I send them to your top producer?"

"Well of course!"

"Who is that?"

Now I'm building a network—the top producer now wants to meet me because I'm going to send him qualified buyers!

Wright

Tom, you are the only sales trainer I know who talks about a "No" close to clients who feel that they have to say "no." What is the "No" close?

Hopkins

David, that's funny that you'd ask because the "No" close is really an advanced close, meaning that it's not for a brand new person—it's for that person who's been out there many years in sales, and they know that there will be people right there in the beginning who have got to say "no" and you're wasting your time. The basic "No" close allows them to say "no," but the no will mean a "yes."

Let me say something and then you just say, "Tom, I just have to say no." Ready?

"David, I really feel that these financial services will be good for you and your family."

Wright

"Tom, I just have to say no."

Hopkins

"Well you know, David, there are many salespeople in the world and they all seem to have opportunities that they're confident that are good for you, and of course they have some persuasive reasons for you to invest in them, haven't they? You of course can say no to any or all of them, can't you? But you see, as a professional with my financial services, my experiences have taught me an overwhelming truth: no one can say 'no' to me. All they can say 'no' to is themselves and their company's future financial security. Tell me, David, how can I accept that kind of 'no'? In fact, if you were me, would you let me say 'no' to anything so critical to the company's future financial gain?"

Wright

That is great.

Hopkins

And you'd say, "No, no I wouldn't," which is why it's a "No" closer. I'm the only one who teaches that. I'm also telling the people, "Listen, Ace, they recorded that. You really have to know what you're doing and be a pro. Ace, you have to have the guts to try it." In fact, that's the truth of all closing skills—you have to have the guts to continue with the attitude, "What do I have to lose? Let's try one more word, one more phrase, and maybe I can take a 'no' into a yes!"

Wright

You have said that your years of experience with millions of salespeople have proven to you that the top people have one important characteristic in common: they are good listeners. Most people think salespeople have the "gift of gab." Would you explain the difference?

Hopkins

Most salespeople do have a gift of gab. In a way they are talkative and communicative; but they need to learn the discipline of shutting up and asking questions. If you're the opposite of what the buyer expects—meaning I'm not a big talker, I'm a better listener—I'll start off my presentation by having in essence four or five questions.

For example, I might say, "David, before I talk to you about advertising with our radio station, it's not fair for me to tell you what we can do until I find out if you really have a need for our service because I don't want to waste your time. Can I ask you a couple questions? Who are you using now for your advertising?" I'll find out what your past experiences are with my questions and then I'll find out what you enjoyed about what you've been doing with these companies. Then I'll find out what changes you'd like to make, and eventually I'll open your mind up with questions. The prospect might then ask me, "Why don't you write up what you can do for us to see if we might want to consider it?" That's the whole key—get that little door open and I'll open the whole company for my business.

Wright

In an article about listening, you advocate questioning and encouraging others. Instead of being pushy, you suggest a salesman be "pulling." What do you mean by "pulling"?

Hopkins

Pushy means I make a statement like, "David, we are the best! You should do business with us!" That's a statement. A question is, "David, we spent years developing our rapport with customers and clients like you, and you agree with me that if we're professional and can help you, then it might make sense to look into what we can do for you." You see the difference? The statement: "We're the best, you need what we can do, you should buy this," is a sentence that contains all statements. The pro thinks about, "How can I make it a question?"

Here's another example of pulling: "Now I just want to ask you this, David: I know you're probably very financially well off, but if I can show you how to retire eight years sooner with ten times more money than you have right now, would you at least listen to what I have to say?"

Wright

That does make sense!

Hopkins

It does! And that's a great sentence, by the way. To you guys and gals in sales: everything must not only make sense, but it must trigger your prospects' desire to know more and be curious about what you can do for them.

Wright

The first time I met you we talked about real estate. I was running a real estate company in Tennessee and you had a great selling program. Five years after that my company was closing eleven hundred single-family dwellings. Today that would be about 150 million dollars. Your record of helping people grow is outstanding.

Who taught you the principles you now teach and helped you get to where you are today?

Hopkins

The very first person was my mother. My mother was a wonderful woman who treated people so beautifully. She would come home after going out to dinner with a couple and she'd sit down and write a thank you note. That's where I first learned about thank notes—from my mom! She also had a wonderful attitude of gratitude—she was very thankful, she thanked God for her blessings. She was a very spiritual woman and she passed that on to me.

Then of course I met people who were top producers. They were not interested in the money as much as making people happy and making clients happy. There's nothing greater than selling a product, making a fee and income, and then having them thank you for doing it for them! That's when you really are great.

Wright

So what do you see on the horizon for those who would choose sales as a career? Will sales always be a rewarding and exciting career for people just starting out in business?

Hopkins

I believe that selling is the lowest paid "easy" work, and the highest paid "hard" work in the world.

New people in sales have to put a commitment of two or three years of building their business until it's all referrals, but there's nothing better than being in business for yourself! And I will say this: the average American wants to own their own business and wants to be in charge of their destiny, but most people don't have the ability or the money to open up a big company because they don't have the cash to say, "Here's $150,000."

You can find a company with a great product that you really believe in. That's the key—you must love the product, you must believe in the product. The reason I did so well in real estate is I totally believed that real estate is the foundation of this entire country's financial base, and the folks who own more real estate will have more net worth and so forth. You've got to believe in what you sell.

To all of our readers: find a product you love and believe in; give up a paycheck and learn the profession of selling! I can teach you every word to say, and then you'll be amazed at how much money you can make.

Wright

Lastly, what is in the future for Tom Hopkins? Where do you go from here after all your successes?

Hopkins

I'm asked that often. Many people have been with me in my training sessions for twenty-five to thirty years. They say, "Hey, you don't have to leave Scottsdale, Arizona, and do a seminar! Why do you still go out and do it?" I've got to say this (and I hope people grab this): if you have a talent to do something that helps your fellow man, and God's blessed you with that, I believe that you have an obligation to do it!

To retire at my age and sit back and play golf every day, although I could, I don't believe that's what I should do. I think I spent twenty-five to thirty years building a reputation. Now, when I come into most cities all the seminars are selling out because people say, "Hopkins teaches the truth and what really works in closing sales!" So I really believe that my future is to train more people than any other person.

Let me give you an example, David. There's been no human being who has done 5,000 seminars in his or her career. I'm at 4,576 right now. My goal before I die is to say, "I did 5,000 seminars!" Then I'll feel that my legacy and my talents have been used. All those people I've touched have had the chance to have better lives, more income, and more growth. If I've done that, I think I have achieved what I'm supposed to achieve as a human being.

Wright

You don't mind if I go home and tell my wife that you said it's okay for me to keep working?

Hopkins

Yes, yes—let her know that we are both going to keep working!

Wright

Absolutely—this is what I'm supposed to be doing!

Hopkins

That's right! David, just remember that "working" is something you're doing when you'd rather do something else. My life has *never* been work. When I was in real estate it wasn't "work," I loved it! When I get up on the stage and do my seminars, I'm not "working"—I am helping people financially grow. So if you're still "working," find something you love to do where the money isn't important—something you just *love* to do and do it!

Wright

What a great conversation. I always enjoy talking with you. I always go away from our conversations thinking I can do anything in the world.

Hopkins

Well, thank you, David. I enjoyed talking with you again. All the best to those reading this!

Wright

We've been talking today with Tom Hopkins who is a sales legend. His credibility with me lies in his track record. He's proud of that track record—he has trained over 3,000,000 students on five continents, and he has shared the stage with some of the great, great speakers and leaders of our time.

Tom, thank so much for being with us today on *Conversations on Success*.

About the Author

Tom Hopkins is a sales legend. Many believe that natural ability is enough to make you successful in a selling career. The truth of the matter is that natural skill, combined with "how to" training is the real secret to high level productivity. Having learned this lesson the hard way, Tom is quick to admit that his early sales career was not successful. After benefiting from professional training, he became a dedicated student, internalizing and refining sales techniques which enabled him to become the sales leader in his industry.

Tom Hopkins
www.TomHopkins.com

Chapter Three

An interview with . . .

Joeann Fossland

David Wright (Wright)

Today we're talking with Joeann Fossland. As Chief Evolution Officer of Advantage Solutions Group, LLC, Joeann uses her passion and creativity to serve others by delivering keynotes, coaching, workshops, and articles. Her purpose is to ignite within the people she touches their own creativity and drive so they can have awesome business success and are able to live a life they love. She writes a weekly e-mail newsletter and has an award-winning blog. You can visit her at www.Joeann.com.

Joeann, welcome to *Conversations on Success!*

Joeann Fossland (Fossland)

Thank you, David; I'm delighted to be here.

Wright

How do you define success?

Fossland

I think for every individual that's unique. Personally, I have a simple version, and a version that is a little bit longer. My simple version is just that I'm successful if I experience joy every day. My longer version is that success is having the resources, the health, the energy, the money, and the time to wake up every day and do what you want to do. What could be better than that?

Unfortunately, some people confuse joy and happiness. So, when I say "experience joy every day," I think joy is really that passion that comes from within you, whereas happiness is sometimes an elusive outer feeling we strive for. What I've found is that successful people separate the way they feel from their capacity to be satisfied and have joy. They know that they have the ability at any time, under all circumstances, to change the way they feel.

Wright

Who were your role models or mentors when designing a successful life for yourself, and what did you learn from them?

Fossland

Parents are often the major role models, and both of my parents filled that role for me. My father was a super-successful salesperson, and I've always loved sales because of the passion he had. But my mother was really the one who gave me a lot of my thinking about success. She encouraged me to take risks and not play it too safe. First of all, she told me not to be like everybody else. That was the perfect message in the '60s and '70s when I was growing up because that's what they were all saying. In those years, we were finding our way as unique individuals—the hippies and living alternative lifestyles. Many mothers had a conversation like this: "Just because Johnny can do it, it doesn't mean that you have to do it. Don't be like everyone else." For some reason, that concept stuck with me. What I was really able to take from that was a uniqueness that was part of me. Turning myself into a clone of someone else was not going to be where I got the most joy. So the joy was in being who I really was.

Another lesson she taught me (and this one's very simple) was to ask myself, "What have you got to lose?" I was eleven years old when I first had a conversation with her about risk-taking. We were in a department store having lunch and there were models sashaying through the lunch room decked out in the latest fashions. I noticed that were no child models—only grown-ups. I said to her, "You know, they could really make a lot of money because everybody's shopping for back-to-school stuff. What they need is some kid's clothes being modeled here!"

"We need to go right upstairs and tell the manager that," she said.

I said, "Really?"

"Sure!" she replied. "What have we got to lose? Who do you think would be a good model?"

"Well, that would be fun," I said. "I'd love to do that!"

So off we went to see the manager. As the doors in the elevator were about to open, I turned to her and said, "Do you really think this is a good idea?"

"What have you got to lose?" she answered.

That question has stuck with me from that time on each time I consider asking somebody for something or taking a step into unfamiliar territory where I don't know if I'm qualified but I know it's something I want to do.

That day went very well because the manager was fairly surprised to see an eleven-year-old come up to his desk and propose something in a respectful and thoughtful manner. He handed me an application to fill out! While I wasn't hired, the very next year they had teen models.

My mother always told me, "You can do anything you really want to do!" I was lucky enough—at least I look back on it as luck—to be able to go to an all girl's school. I think that there's a trend these days to always make everything equal for both sexes, but in the girls' school there was certainly something special about not having compete against the boys as a little girl. In that girls' school, they also told us we could do anything we wanted. I believe the messages we give to out kids are critically important in developing the self-image they have.

My mom died when I was fifteen. It was really tough. I loved this woman and respected her. I learned so much from her and yet she left me a legacy as I witnessed her live each day fully. She had been diagnosed with a fatal disease ten years earlier and they told her she had three to four years to live. She took very good care of herself and lived for ten more years. I know that was because she wanted to be there for my brother and me. Through those years she rarely complained, she lived each day fully, and gave me the gift of learning how to live for today. Most people don't know when they are going to die. The reality is that we could suddenly be hit by a car or, heaven forbid, something like 9/11 happens. Through the years, knowing how precious each day is has made me say "yes" to things I otherwise might not have done had I played it safe. I am acutely aware that this might be my only opportunity to see somebody for the last time or to do something for the last time. So I've made it a point not to hold back, to always tell people I love them as though it might be the very last time I have to see them. We say that a lot in my family.

Wright

Would you give our readers some examples of ways you have actually pursued success?

Fossland

I've always been somebody who enjoys achievement. As I work with my coaching clients, I find that when one is tapped into one's core values, there's a certain passion that naturally expresses itself. Having a core value of achievement has made me jump into many things that didn't have a guaranteed positive outcome. I am driven to try something when someone says I can't do it. I love a challenge. I worked hard in school and was the valedictorian of my high school class.

A few years ago I had a friend who was diagnosed with hepatitis C. She had asked me if I could pledge money because she was going to run a triathlon the Arizona Liver Foundation was organizing to raise money for the Liver Foundation.

"Yes, sure," I replied, "I'll donate," and in my next breath I said, "Could I run it with you?"

I have to tell you, I'm not a runner. I had never run even five hundred yards in my life before that, but I was so touched that she was going to do this with hepatitis C that I jumped in with her. And from that moment I started thinking about ways we could make it a win-win. Being a businesswoman I have a fairly large database of people who subscribe to my coaching tips and come to the places where I speak, so I thought it would be very easy for me to raise the money I needed. That was in 2002, and I raised nearly $5,000 in ten-, fifteen-, and twenty-dollar contributions. That was really exciting.

Aside from raising the money, it was exciting to finish the mini-triathlon, which involved running five miles, hiking three, and riding a bike for ten miles. At fifty-four I was the oldest woman there. There was one man who was older, but most of them were kids in their twenties and thirties who were saying, "Isn't this fun?" I'll tell you though, five or six hours of continuous energy in exercise is *not* my idea of fun! My idea of fun is a margarita on a beach! But there was a definite feeling of success as I crossed the finish line.

Another thing that I'm proud having done is supporting *More* magazine's drive to raise a million dollars for CARE, the humanitarian organization that is doing incredible work in raising the living standards for people all over the world. *More* had created a challenge for "Giving Circles." A Giving Circle is a group of people who join together to pool their resources and energy to make a difference. And in my mind I thought, "Wow, if twenty people each raised $5,000 in our Giving Circle, and nine other Giving Circles each raised $100,000, *More* could get to their million." So, I e-mailed all my friends and people I respected and asked them to join with me and pledge to raise $5,000. It seemed reasonable, given I could do what I did with the Liver Foundation.

I took on the project and we called it "The Web Women Giving Circle." While we didn't hit our goal, we raised close to $25,000. That was more than any other. We won a free trip to Peru this year with the people from Care and were privileged to see all the work they are doing down there to empower people. I'm pretty excited about that; it was certainly a success. We are going to raise the rest to make our goal this year. Sometimes things don't happen in the timeframe you expect or want. The universe has its own timeline, but we aren't taking our eyes off the goal.

Wright

What do you think about the word "success" as it relates to people to finding it for themselves, and has it changed?

Fossland

I do think it has changed in the past few years. I think 9/11 had something to do with that. People began to realize how precious each day is. I also think generationally a lot of the Gen-Xers and Gen-Ys don't want to be workaholics. They are just as concerned with their own personal lives working as well as their careers. I believe more and more that people are defining success not as solely their business achievement, but as whether or not they have life balance—they have lives they love to lead. Their careers may also be flourishing, but it's not at the expense of their personal lives.

In the '90s (and you can probably relate to this), there were many people who were workaholics, trying so hard to be the best, which is great, but if you're doing that at the expense of your personal life, you get burned out. I believe there has been a shift; it's no longer a badge of honor to say, "I'm working sixty hours a week or twelve hours a day," I think most people these days want balance in their lives.

Wright

What do you mean when you say, "Life is too short to perfect your weaknesses"?

Fossland

That's one of my favorite things to tell people! I find that most people focus on what they don't do well, and then they strive to do it better instead of using their natural strengths to leverage what is easiest in which to excel. Don't you find that when you do something well, it's easy to work on it and do it better? I know that is true for most people. Yet, most people gravitate toward fixing their weaknesses.

For instance, if someone is not good at numbers, he or she will say, "Oh, I should take a course and get better doing this." When I work with my coaching clients, we will focus on their best strengths because that's how they can leverage themselves and work smarter instead of harder. Then they must delegate or let go of their weaknesses so they don't drain time they could be spending on something in which they're really brilliant.

Wright

What qualities do you see that distinguish being successful from the ordinary?

Fossland

I think there are quite a few of them. The most important quality I have found in people who are successful is their attitude. I don't just mean positive thinking—I find people who are really successful have a *passion*. Their belief in what they *want* to do is exceptionally contagious most of the time. It leads them to do things with other people and attract others to them. They have a clear vision about what they want.

People who aren't as successful often haven't taken the time to develop the clarity in what's important to them and what they want the end vision to look like. From that clarity of vision, successful people have an intention—they will look for the evidence of what *is* working, rather than evidence that tells them "you can't do this." They look at everything that happens as a stepping-stone to get to where they want, and they keep their eye on that vision and that intention.

People who are successful have a strong self-image. Earlier I shared some of the ideas my mother taught me. I am so grateful to her for the self-confidence building that she gave me. I'm trying to do that right now with my five-year-old granddaughter. I believe it is important to let her know she *can* do anything.

Successful people have a core strength of believing in themselves. I think this is something that people can change and can learn if they didn't get encouragement when they were young; but it may take work and conscious effort.

Another quality I find really important for a successful person is that successful people take responsibility for everything. Even if they have circumstances that aren't conducive to taking them to where they want to go, they will take responsibility and say, "I can do something about this!" and they own it.

The last quality, and maybe the most important, is that successful people take action. Ordinary people "think about it," they plan, and take a lot of time before they get to the point of being ready to jump in, but successful people are willing to go forward.

Wright

When working with your coaching clients, how do you discover what success is for them?

Fossland

I find that most people don't think much about this. Wouldn't it be great if in college or even high school, we had a class on life planning—looking at what you want to be when you grow up? A course like that would help kids give some serious thought to what they want their lives to be about, and what *would* be successful for them.

One of my other mentors was Thomas Leonard who started the virtual university called Coach U that was started in the early 1990s when virtual universities were unheard of. Thomas said, "You can't get enough of what you really don't want." The first time I heard him say that I was perplexed and wondered what he was talking about. He gave us an example of a woman who wanted her husband to give her jewelry and fabulous gifts for her birthday or Christmas, but those things were not really want she wanted. What she really wanted was love or appreciation.

We often use these outer trappings to tell us that that a person loves us, and yet no amount of jewelry is going to be enough if you don't really get the love you want. What I learned from this is that there is a feeling inside all of us that is as insatiable as a black hole if we aren't getting what is really important to us. We try to do more or buy more things that to show we're successful, and yet nothing is ever enough.

When I work with my clients, the first thing we talk about is core values so that I can get a better sense of what is really important to them. Is it family? Is it community? Is it appreciation? Is it achievement? What are the core values that drive them? As I said in the beginning, the definition of success is unique to each person. Establishing core values is a way to discover what people are passionate about. From there, I work with their definition of success because, as a coach, I don't believe I have the right to tell anybody else what success should be. I think there are many people walking around who have been told what success should be, so when coaching my clients I joke about this by saying, "They're shoulding all over themselves!"

Wright

What gets in the way of people finding success?

Fossland

First of all, what gets in the way is confusion about knowing or not knowing what's really important to them. Secondly, it's often chasing the wrong things. They don't have clarity of what's really going to make them joyful.

Let's revisit the distinction between joy and happiness. People often have quite a few things that for a very short term will make them happy—things like a new car or a new "toy" they've just bought. But this kind of happiness wears off quickly. They then chase after the next new thing, unaware of what they really need.

Thirdly, I believe most people are often too hard on themselves. People have to believe in themselves. Many people look at what they don't have and what they can't do, and they look at their weaknesses. They beat themselves up about that and they don't enjoy what *is* working.

We live in this amazingly rich country here in the United States where we have more on average than 95 percent of the people in the world. The trip I did with Care to Peru underscored that for me. In Peru we saw several villages where the people seem so happy in spite of their poverty. They're living on less than two dollars a day, and yet they have families, they have a little piece of land they are working, and I saw joy in their faces.

I think what often gets in the way is that people have these pictures of what somebody told them success should be and those images just don't fit with their definition based upon their core values. They compare themselves with others and will find themselves unable to measure up

The last thing I find that gets in the way of success is not having a big enough vision. We need things that bring forth our passion; we need things that are aligned with our core values that we get *excited* about. Many people seem to be just trying to get through the day instead of realizing what a precious day it is and that they are still above ground. We must embrace our dreams and chase them!

Wright

What are some of the strategies or tools you use with your clients to help them be more successful?

Fossland

I find often when my clients are stuck or they are not having the experience of success, they are disconnected from their core values. Bringing their core values into whatever they are doing will bring that passion back. When I notice there's a struggle, we'll go back and have a conversation about core values: What's really important to you? How can you bring more of that into what you're doing every day?

Sometimes we're in a job or we're in a situation with others that we can't change, but at any time we can change our perception of whether something is good or bad. We can change our perception of whether we making a difference here—we can actually shift the "who we're being" instead of "what we're doing." So when my clients are stuck, we'll examine how they can shift their thinking rather than doing "more, harder, faster"—more, harder, faster these days usually isn't a good solution.

The second strategy I often use is creating more gratitude. I ask clients to make a list every day of the things that they are grateful for. I ask them to concentrate for just a few minutes a day on what they're grateful for and that shifts their internal energy.

Internal energy is what attracts people to us, and it attracts events and wonderful things to us. Without that energy, we are repulsive. What we think about expands. If we think "there is not enough," that's what is manifested. I know this concept isn't new. When we are conscious every day about what we are thinking, we begin to see why we're stuck. Our thinking brings that scarcity into our life or brings us to a determination where we think we really *can't* do what we say we want to do or be successful.

So gratitude grounds you in what *is* working and what you do have, and shifts the energy to enable you to appreciate that more.

The last tool I often use with clients is something I call "Ten Delicious Daily Habits." I ask my clients to come up with ten things they'll do for themselves each and every day. This is magical because it's not ten *more* things they have to put on their to-do list, but it involves small things that will nurture them or make them feel that they are taking care of themselves.

One woman put on her list, "Listen to the sound of my children's laughter." Isn't that wonderful? I just loved that. It wasn't a to-do that would make her do more, but it involved her being present in the moment.

One of mine is, "Go out and watch the sunset"—just to take five minutes at the end of the day, take some deep breaths, and live in that moment. We have gorgeous sunsets out here in Tucson, and I want to appreciate this wonderful universe I live in and the opportunities I have.

Others habits to include on the list might be simple things like, "Drink my eight glasses of water" or "Take my vitamins." I find that this is like the story about the airplane where we're told to put on our oxygen mask before we help somebody else. In my seminars I ask, "Why do they tell you to do that?"

Audience members will usually reply, "Well, if you don't have oxygen going to your brain, you can't think."

"Exactly!" I reply. "Have you ever noticed how many people are walking around without oxygen going to their brains?"

I see over-worked people who are really striving so hard, and they are afraid to get off the hamster wheel they're running on to take care of themselves first. I believe the hallmark of successful people is that they take great care of themselves so that they can serve others. They know they're actually a model for other people as well. So when they're living successfully, other people are going to want to emulate what they're doing. People need to take very, very good care of themselves so they have energy and health and are able to touch other people.

Wright

So as you look down the road, what's next for Joeann Fossland?

Fossland

I am so grateful to I have the opportunity to speak in front of more and more people. I feel so blessed to be able to spread joy. My intention is to continue to help people, hoping that out of an interaction with me they will be more in touch with how they can have more joy in their lives.

About the Author

A sought after-speaker and coach, Joeann Fossland uses her passion and creativity to serve others by delivering keynotes, one-on-one and group coaching, workshops, and articles. She strives to ignite within the people she touches their own creativity and drive so they can have awesome business success and are able to live lives they love. She writes a weekly e-mail newsletter and has an award winning blog.

Joeann Fossland
Advantage Solutions Group, LLC
PO Box 133
Cortaro, AZ 85652
Phone: 520.744.8731
E-mail: joeann@joeann.com
www.Joeann.com

Chapter Four

An interview with . . .

Sue Becker

David Wright (Wright)

Today we are talking with organizational consultant Sue Becker, founder and owner of From Piles to Smiles.™ Sue's company assists business and residential clients in living more stress-free and harmoniously by helping them reduce clutter, organize paperwork, and manage their time.

Sue is also a professional speaker to corporations, hospitals, and organizations around the country. Thousands of individuals have benefited from her services, experiencing the joy and peacefulness that comes from feeling in control and having more time to enjoy what matters in life.

Sue's professional memberships include the National Study Group on Chronic Disorganization (treasurer and Illinois' first Certified Professional Organizer in Chronic Disorganization) and the National Association of Professional Organizers (former vice president of the Chicago chapter). Her writings have appeared in over seventy periodicals and books including: *Real Simple* magazine and *How to Position Yourself as the Obvious Expert*. Sue also appeared as an organizational expert on NBC News and the national television show, *Starting Over*.

Sue, a CPA, has also earned an MBA from Northwestern University's Kellogg Graduate School of Management.

Sue, welcome to *Conversations on Success*.

Sue Becker (Becker)

Thank you, David; it's great to be here.

Wright

How do you define success?

Becker

I think success revolves around having a meaningful and fulfilling life and the realization of having achieved that. You start each day with optimism and passion, and end it knowing that what you did that day really matters. It matters to you; it could matter to your loved ones; it could matter to your community; it could matter more broadly in the world. At any point in your life you want to be able to say, "I am the best person I can be." We all have different gifts and one person's picture of success will not look like anyone else's. That's why I think it's important to look at a process of discovering who we are uniquely meant to be. We should be proud of who we are and who we are becoming. Most of all, we need to *love* who we are. When we do that, we are successful.

Wright

What would you say are the biggest contributors to your professional success?

Becker

Clearly defined goals, self-discipline, organization, faith, and courage have significantly contributed to my success. I have a clear idea of what's important to me and have organized my life around those things. *Self-discipline* helps me stay focused on what's important and prevents me from getting off track—at least not too much. Good *organization skills* allow me to lay out a clear path of what I need to do to get where I want to go. This includes organizing my time as well as my physical space.

My *faith* has summoned me to listen to God. He guides me to advance with *courage* in times of uncertainty, which has included leaving a secure, well-paying job to start my own business. I've been able to take a leap of faith, trusting that I'm always moving closer to becoming the person I was meant to be.

Wright

What are common traits of successful people?

Becker

Successful people definitely know what's important to them. They have a clearly defined purpose for their life and a specific plan to help them achieve their purpose. That includes writing down the steps of this plan so they can focus on them every day. Successful people pursue what is meaningful to them by constantly asking, "Is this leading me toward my goals?" Life is all about choices. We're wise to make the right choices that lead us toward becoming who we are meant be. This goes back to self-discipline. We have good habits and bad habits; to succeed we have to change the habits that stop us and create habits that propel us. Successful people make each moment count by changing whatever might be preventing them from achieving their life's purpose. They manage themselves wisely with respect to time.

Wright

What are some of the biggest time management mistakes people make?

Becker

A lot of people have issues with time management. Often we look for external explanations to know why we can't manage our time. However, the biggest mistake of all is not recognizing that time management is really *self* management. It's not something that is done to us—it's about having the self-discipline to do what's important to help us reach our goals. It's about having the self-discipline to set aside time for unburdened fun as well as for becoming the person we were meant to be.

Other time-management related mistakes people make are not having clearly defined goals, not writing things down, not estimating how long things will take, not prioritizing tasks, and not planning the day clearly. First, if you don't have well-defined goals, then it becomes a time-management issue because you won't know how to spend your time. When no one thing is more important than anything else, you have no direction for your life. It doesn't matter if you're watching television or writing a great novel, you still need clearly defined goals coupled with a plan of action on how to achieve them. Writing down specific steps to complete your plan clarifies intent and turns it into commitment.

After writing things down, then you'd estimate how long each step will take so you know the total amount of time required. From there, you can prioritize your tasks and plan each day according to how much time is needed to complete the most important activities.

Wright

You mentioned prioritizing. That is a huge challenge for lots of people. How do you suggest people prioritize?

Becker

Certainly you make sure that any task you plan to do is important to you. Ask yourself the question: "Is this something that will lead me toward my goals?" Then determine which tasks will give you the "most bang for your buck" in terms of payoff for the time you have invested. This is why it's critical to estimate how long things will take. Otherwise, you could busily spend time doing things that don't lead toward your goals and not leave enough time for your priority tasks.

Of course, you also have to consider deadlines. If something requires having a hard and fast deadline, take that into consideration when you prioritize your activities. Keep in mind that everything doesn't have to be done *now;* look at the "big picture" and recognize that you can put off non-essential things and stay focused on the most critical tasks for the moment. A key question to ask yourself when prioritizing is, "If I could get only one thing done today, what must it be?"

Wright

You mentioned estimating how long things will take when you prioritize. Should that estimate include time to respond to interruptions and phone calls?

Becker

Yes. It's a fact of life that you'll have interruptions. So it makes sense to include time for interruptions and phone calls when estimating how long activities will take. However, if you're working on something time sensitive or extremely important, you have to decide not to allow interruptions and phone calls to take you away from the task at hand.

My preference is to stay focused on the current task, especially when working on something critical. I let my phone calls go to voicemail and set a specific time to go back and check them. When I'm working with a client, I don't answer my cell phone. In fact, I make sure my voicemail message says that when I'm with a client, I do not answer my calls. That way, callers don't expect me to get back to them immediately. We live in a culture where we are expected to respond instantly, so it's better to take control of the situation, exercise self-management, and determine when you'll allow yourself to be interrupted.

Wright

How do you suggest people set up systems or establish habits to prioritize their activities and cut down on interruptions?

Becker

Once you accept that *time management is self-management*, you make the decision to break bad habits and establish new, helpful habits. Using those written goals that I talked about before, simply ask yourself, "Is this moving me closer to my goals?" anytime you consider doing something. You have to make a conscious decision to catch yourself falling into old, bad habits as you work on creating new, good habits. It always helps to write things down.

To establish a habit of prioritizing, place a note for yourself somewhere that you can easily see it—in front of your computer, inside your planner, on your mirror. The note would say, "Am I moving closer to my goals?" and, "What's the most important thing I should be doing right now?"

As for interruptions, we often interrupt ourselves as frequently as external factors interrupt us. For example, we jump from one task to another rather than staying focused. Some people open their e-mails every time the little ding sounds, thinking, "Surely it's something more interesting than whatever I'm currently working on." Similarly, they answer the phone every time it rings.

It's important to set up your own self-management system to establish habits that stop you from giving in to the temptation of interruptions. So when someone interrupts you, you can let that person know you're working on something important and then arrange a later time to speak. Have some predetermined, rehearsed phrases you can say to people in these situations such as, "I'd love to talk to you but I have to finish this by three o'clock. May I call you when I've finished?"

Another strategy is setting aside a fixed amount of time when you don't allow yourself to be interrupted. This can be an hour a day or an hour a week. It's intended to make sure you have *quality time* to focus on important tasks without the threat of being interrupted. It's critical to select tasks that are worthy of this valuable, uninterrupted time so you don't squander it.

What's the key? It's taking charge rather than letting your days be dictated to you. It's also getting comfortable with the knowledge that establishing habits takes time. After all, it took a lifetime to create your current habits, so recognize that you may not change them quickly or easily; but it will be worth it when you do!

Wright

Planning and writing things down are simple organizational concepts, but people struggle with doing them. Will you give us some tips on these? And how does organizing on paper differ from organizing on a computer, PDA, or cell phone?

Becker

Let me first define these two concepts—planning and writing. Writing things down means having a single place to capture ideas and to-do's so you won't forget them. Whether you write in a notebook or on a piece of paper or use an electronic device, you're capturing your ideas in writing. Don't be at the mercy of your memory! Once you have your established place, you can then trust that you'll remember them.

Planning involves identifying priorities and blocking out time to work on those to-do's and ideas you've written down. Writing your lists captures your intentions; planning turns them into commitments.

I suggest including three components when writing things down: 1) write down the idea or activity itself, 2) estimate how long the task will take, and 3) set a deadline for completing it.

First is making sure you break any project or complex task down into its most finite components. This gives you a clear path regarding what you need to do. It also allows you to chip away at doing a big activity in small chunks rather than feeling you have to do it all at once.

Second is determining how long each task will take. People often get into trouble because they identify something they want to do and talk themselves out of it, believing they don't have time to do it right now. Or they start a task intending to finish it in one session, but it takes much longer. If you give yourself a *realistic* time estimate and recognize how much time is needed to block out to complete a task, you'll have much better success getting it done. And finally, giving yourself a deadline for each task is critical. There's no greater motivator than a deadline! Deadlines also help gain perspective on what things are most critical so you can prioritize.

Once you've captured your to-dos and ideas, estimated how long each one will take, and given yourself a deadline for completing each one, it's time to actually plan when to do them. The planning piece involves reviewing your to-do list at least once a week, scheduling items that are a priority, and making sure you'll have time to work on them that week. Write them in your time management tool—your calendar, your planner, your PDA, your phone— whatever works for you. Identify exactly *when* you will do the specific task and write down that time.

You'll find that following these steps gets you to move your intentions to commitments. And these commitments will help you achieve your goals.

Wright

Technology seems to have expanded the volume of work people have rather than shortened their days. How can a successful time manager use technology wisely?

Becker

The stress resulting from information overload is huge because it can prevent people from enjoying their lives. I also think overload causes analysis paralysis because so much information can get in the way of making decisions. Knowing that more information is available, people often put off making decisions. But postponed decision-making can cause a lot of stress and ineffectiveness too. And it certainly wastes a lot of time! So it's wise to give yourself a time limit. No matter how much or how little information you have, when the time is up, make a decision based on the information you have.

Remember, just because more information is available doesn't mean it's necessary for you to gather it all. When do you have enough information to make a decision? Will getting more information add any value to your decision-making process? Answering these questions will compel you to be more efficient with your information-gathering.

For many people, e-mails and cell phone calls control their time. In fact, I've heard news reports about people getting addicted to their e-mails and PDAs. Successful people, though, show great self-discipline regarding their technology tools. They don't let them control their schedule. Instead, they set aside time on their calendars to check phone messages and e-mails. All the while they ask themselves, "What's the most important thing I should be doing right now?"

Wright

If you could give readers one piece of advice on how to be successful, what would it be?

Becker

More than a single piece of advice, I offer this overriding idea: I encourage you to discover a purpose for your life. Then write down the specific goals and the specific tasks you'll use to drive your behavior at any given moment. Honor your commitments to yourself by designing a life that leads you toward that purpose.

It's critical that you take charge and don't let others dictate your days for you. Recognize that some days will be better than others, but as long as you are moving in the right direction, you'll continue toward becoming and loving the person you were meant to be. And that's success.

About the Author

Sue Becker is an organizational consultant and the founder and owner of From Piles to Smiles™. Sue's company helps business and residential clients become who they were meant to be by removing obstacles such as clutter, disorganized paperwork, and poor time management.

Sue is also a professional speaker to corporations, hospitals, and organizations around the country. Thousands of individuals have benefited from Sue's assistance and wisdom, creating substantial changes in their lives that have helped them discover who they are meant to be.

Sue's professional memberships include the National Study Group on Chronic Disorganization (treasurer and Illinois' first Certified Professional Organizer in Chronic Disorganization) and the National Association of Professional Organizers (former vice president of the Chicago chapter). Her writings have appeared in over seventy periodicals and books, including: *Real Simple Magazine* and *How to Position Yourself as the Obvious Expert.* Sue also appeared as an organizational expert on NBC News and the national television show *Starting Over.*

A CPA, Sue has earned an MBA from Northwestern University's Kellogg Graduate School of Management.

Sue Becker, CPO-CD®, ADD Specialist
From Piles to Smiles™
P.O. Box 903
Downers Grove, IL 60515
Phone: 630.724.1111
E-mail: Organized@PilesToSmiles.com
www.PilesToSmiles.com

Chapter Five

An interview with . . .

Duane Cashin

David Wright (Wright)

Today we're talking with Duane Cashin. After thirteen years of business success in companies ranging in size from medium to Fortune 500 and positions from straight commission salesman to Vice President of Sales, Duane decided to start his own company. Within four years Duane's grand format graphics company grew to be a multimillion dollar organization with its work displayed at the Super Bowl, Rockefeller Center, Radio City Music Hall, and MTV's studios at Times Square. His speaking skills were honed when he joined Tony Parinello, author of *Selling to VITO*. Duane sold and delivered these famous seminars throughout the United States while establishing a sales record that is still unbroken.

Duane, welcome to *Conversations on Success!*

Duane Cashin (Cashin)

Thank you, David!

Wright

Is it really as competitive today as people would lead us to believe?

Cashin

I don't think it is. However, I do agree it's very crowded. I find with technology today being readily available and affordable, companies can create a beautiful

Web site and excellent marketing materials virtually overnight. In doing so they are creating a business presence that, at face value, appears to be impressive. They can quickly copy effective elements of a competitor's offering and as a result of this capability, the distinction between brands is beginning to blur. In many markets buyers are finding it difficult to see the differences between one product and service and another. When buyers find themselves in this situation they default to price. We all know how unpleasant selling becomes when our prospect feels there is no difference between us and the competition. It's very disheartening to be told they intend to do business with the "vendor" offering the lowest price!

When we find ourselves in this situation it's natural to feel our marketplace is becoming more and more competitive. The good news is if you can change your perspective and focus on truly delivering value to your prospects and improve your ability to articulate *how* you deliver value, you *can* stand out in the crowd.

Wright

What is the profile of today's sales and service professional?

Cashin

One of the classic sales questions is: "Are top sales professionals born or are they made?" I firmly believe that if you have an individual who is resilient, articulate, committed to self-development, and who has an above average energy level, you can create a top producer through training and support.

In addition to these four traits there is a thought style that separates the weak or average performer from the star. The top performers think and act like businesspeople and not salespeople. Salespeople are self-focused. Their thoughts and actions are largely directed toward making commission dollars. I agree it's important for a salesperson to be money motivated, however, to be exclusively focused on making money does not end up creating value in the eyes of the buyer.

A businessperson, on the other hand, focuses on creating long-term relationships and improving the client condition in some meaningful fashion. This approach stands the test of time and does end up delivering value to the buyer. The sale professionals who are truly successful today have a good general understanding of business—how profits are generated and where costs lie. They understand a bit about finance and a little bit about efficiency. And they possess a sincere empathy for others. They genuinely care about other people and their businesses and they want to help. I find them to be emotionally strong, and what I mean by that is they are resilient—rejection does not wear them down. They know it is part of the process and they can cope with it. They've got a high energy level and they have learned to leverage change to their benefit. They see change as a competitive advantage, they are very curious, and they love to learn. I think if a person has those traits today, with some training and guidance they can become a top performer in business.

Wright

Many businesspeople feel their product and/or service is being viewed as a commodity. What is your opinion of this trend?

Cashin

From the buyer's perspective there is clearly a trend toward commoditization today. Thousands of buyers were asked in a recent survey the following question: "When buying a product, would you like to eliminate the salesperson from the transaction?" I was shocked to learn that 85 percent said, "Yes." Obviously, if the buyer sees no need to have a salesperson involved in the buying process, the buyer's opinion is that the salesperson is not bringing value to the experience. As we discussed earlier, the buyer will now default to price and as a result the product or service will be viewed as a commodity.

If you look closely at these situations, typically you will find that the salesperson is attempting to leverage the features of his or her product in an effort to capture the attention of the buyer and convince the buyer to buy the product. In taking the "product" approach salespeople are actually directing the prospect to view the product as a commodity.

I recently asked a CEO of a $40 million a year company if he would appreciate it if he never got another phone call or e-mail from a salesperson again.

He responded, "I don't have time for a sales pitch but I do have time to learn."

I then asked him when he does give some of his time to a salesperson, what did that salesperson do to earn that opportunity? He explained that the salesperson very quickly displayed that he or she had some insight into his world. He went on to say the salesperson's questions will be relevant and give him visibility into the salesperson's depth of knowledge. The CEO explained that this all happens in about thirty to one hundred and twenty seconds. When salespeople present themselves in this fashion, the CEO explained, he will take the time meet with them. Buyers don't want to deal with salespeople. However, they do want to meet with businesspeople.

Wright

What is more effective in motivating buyers to buy today: promises of their situation being better or ideas to eliminate threats?

Cashin

The approach that most salespeople take today is to "pitch" the virtues of their "product" or "service." The majority of companies today do a great job in product training and a very poor job in "business training." Typically, a buyer's primary focus is to eliminate certain barriers and roadblocks that are standing between him or her and corporate or personal success. Once those needs are satisfied, then buyers typically become interested in knowing what new opportunities your product or service provides.

Unfortunately, most salespeople don't invest the time to study and understand the business issues their prospects deal with, nor are they clear on how their product or service addresses them. In the absence of understanding this, the salesperson defaults to "shallow selling" and making statements like: "This is the best product in its class," or, "Our customers love how it works and they are very pleased with the results." Self-promoting statements like these will not differentiate you from the competition or earn you credibility in your prospects' eyes. In fact, this approach in selling is one of the reasons buyers feel salespeople are not bringing value to the buying experience.

I highly recommend salespeople spend the time necessary to gain insight into, and be able to explain, the consequences a prospect will face when certain situations are left unattended. When you have developed the vision and ability to explain what can go wrong in a prospect's business it will have the effect of elevating your position of credibility. But it must be explained in such a way that you are not perceived as negative or manipulative.

Perhaps it will help if you imagine a doctor—one with good bedside manner of course—explaining to you that it is important for you to lower your cholesterol. If you resist his or her suggestion of taking medication, the doctor might explain the possible consequences you will realize down the road by ignoring his or her advice. When presented in an effective manner, the doctor will be successful in communicating that he or she genuinely cares about your wellbeing. This goes a long way in establishing credibility and melting your resistance!

Wright

What is your opinion of solution- and consultative-based selling?

Cashin

I think they can be very, very powerful. However, the reality is that very few salespeople establish the credibility required to be viewed as a "consultant" or a person whose suggested solutions should be taken seriously. We need to remember that in essence, when a buyer buys from us the buyer is taking our advice. We do not take anyone's advice unless we find him or her to be credible and we trust the person. Just because I have a driver's license doesn't mean I can gain respect on a NASCAR track. Just because you read a book on consultative selling doesn't mean you will earn respect and trust in the eyes of your prospects. If we are to be viewed as trusted advisors we must demonstrate that we have knowledge, insight, and a sincere desire to make the experience all about the prospect.

It is truly amazing how quickly you can differentiate yourself from your competition in the eyes of prospects when you demonstrate you have an understanding of their business operation, their marketplace, and the customers they serve. Studying with the intent on gaining these insights is how we begin the transition from thinking and acting like "salespeople" to that of "businesspeople."

Wright

You have a saying "Get your ACT together!" What exactly do you mean by that?

Cashin

Yes, we should all strive in our business dealings to have our "ACT" together! "ACT" is an acronym that I've created to help us remember the three most important elements of doing business. The A stands for Alignment, the C stands for Credibility, and the T stands for Trust.

When I work with salespeople I suggest to them that they develop their ability to establish alignment with their prospects as early in the relationship as possible. Alignment is created when we demonstrate two things to our prospects: 1) that your relationship will be all about *them,* and 2) that you have an understanding of what it is like to walk in their shoes. This can be accomplished by *very* briefly explaining to your prospect that you are a "specialist" in your area and recently you have made some observations in your prospect's marketplace that he or she may find useful. Some of the areas your prospect will find of interest will be:

- Changes in the prospect's particular marketplace
- News about the prospect's competition
- Comments made by companies or individuals who purchase the prospect's products

You will create alignment with your prospects when it becomes apparent to them you understand *some* of the business concerns and worries that wake them up at 3:00 AM.

Once you have established alignment with your prospect you have paved the way to establishing credibility. In essence, you established alignment by telling your prospect a very short *relevant* story about his or her marketplace, competition, and/or clients. Now you will establish credibility in your prospect's eyes by taking your communication to a deeper level by asking him or her meaningful questions focused in those same areas.

The quickest way for us to gauge people's depth of knowledge and interest in a particular area is by the questions they ask. Your credibility will be established when you illustrate to them you have depth as a businessperson.

Of course, in order for you to have insight into their business you will have to become and remain a student of business. Unfortunately, if you were to observe how most salespeople go about establishing credibility you would see them becoming a virtual waterfall spewing information about their products and themselves in a series of run-on sentences. Here's a secret: If our primary strategy is "telling" prospects what we know, two things happen: number one, they doubt it, and number two, their eyes glaze over and they very quickly become bored. We must trust that if we ask meaningful, relevant, and insightful questions, we will in fact earn credibility.

Let me give you an example of a poor question to ask. I held a workshop for a publishing company that owns several business journals and magazines. Before the workshop began I was interviewing one of the publishers to gain some insight into her operation. I asked, "As it pertains to your perfect prospects, what is their annual revenue?"

There was a long pause. Then the publisher said, "Duane, that's not the right question."

"What is the right question?" I asked.

She said, "A good question to ask me is: what *types* of businesses are your perfect prospects in?" She went on to explain that the organizations that advertise in her magazine are: law firms, dentist offices, wine shops, and clothing stores. She explained it's not their annual revenue that makes them good candidates; it's what business they're in and who they are trying to reach.

What happened when I asked that question? I demonstrated to her in a split second that I didn't understand her business! That's how quickly it happens. We need to understand what it is like to walk in our prospects' shoes. We need to have a basic understanding of what they do and the challenges they face. When we ask relevant and meaningful questions, we send a very clear and *immediate* message to our prospect that we get it. This earns credibility in their eyes.

The last gate we need to pass through is trust. It's an interesting thing—when we have established trust we don't need five tricky closing questions to wrap up the deal. The sale is closed in an effortless gesture of acceptance. Trust is earned only after we have aligned ourselves with the prospect and earned credibility. Once those two gates are passed through we have effectively set the stage to give our opinion and offer the prospect advice. Now when we deliver our proposal and successfully illustrate that our solution has addressed most of their important concerns in language that aligns with the way they think and do business, we pass through the final gate of trust. You are now a trusted advisor and have earned a new client!

Wright

How does "creativity" fit into a hard-driving, "numbers" focused business world?

Cashin

I believe that creativity is really one of the few sustainable competitive advantages we have today. To effectively leverage creativity we have to keep in mind that it is directly linked to emotion.

Years ago in the boardroom you had to be very careful when bringing up the issue of emotion. In performance reviews you would be expected to stick to the numbers exclusively. Today, with more and more competitors in your space, all with professional Web sites and offering similar products all priced pretty much the same, how are you going to differentiate your offering and organization? Solely through the numbers? No! Gain insight and leverage the role emotion plays in business success. Emotion can give you a distinct advantage. It's interesting to note that so many aspects of how people buy have changed over the last ten years. But one thing that has not changed is the fact that buyers buy based on emotion and justify their decision with logic. That's been true for centuries.

So how can you leverage this fact to your advantage? Work very hard and smart to understand what is meaningful to your buyers. Work to understand not only what their business objectives are but perhaps more importantly, strive to understand what is important to them "personally." When you have this insight, you can then design and adjust your questions and presentations to directly hit what is personally important to them. So as your competition is pushing the prospect further and further away by spewing features and making all sorts of patronizing promises of how better off the prospect's company will be as a result of selecting their product, you are connecting to the mind and emotions of your prospects, drawing them closer and closer to your ideas and solutions.

Wright

To most businesspeople a referral is considered to be the most effective prospecting tool available. Is it possible to realize some of the advantages a referral offers in the absence of a referral?

Cashin

Absolutely—if we look at what's at play in a referral: its credibility and trust. When I refer you to another businessperson I have a relationship with, in essence, the message I'm sending is that you bring value to the table; as a result you are credible and you can be trusted. This immediately accomplishes two things for you: Number one, you've instantly gotten past all the gatekeepers. Number two, the prospect will welcome you into his or her business life and listen to what you have to say. The rest is up to you.

So the question is, how can we shorten our visit with the gatekeepers and how can we shorten the path to credibility and trust without the benefit of a personal introduction? You will accomplish this by demonstrating you are knowledgeable, articulate, and that you are all about them.

I suggest you begin your sales process by calling into the C-suite and leverage TITO! TITO is an acronym that stands for: Trends, Issues, Threats, and Opportunities. There are several irrefutable truths in business that you can exploit to your benefit. I mentioned one already—people buy emotionally and justify their decision logically. The second one is the fact that leaders are constantly on the lookout for insights into their marketplace and any ideas that will give them a competitive advantage. Leaders get the big bucks because they can see into the future and aptly apply their vision to making profitable decisions. You can count on this being true.

So how do you leverage this fact to create the elements of credibility and trust when you are calling cold? By understanding the trends that your prospects are facing in their marketplaces. When you demonstrate your understanding of the trends to a leader you can quickly capture his or her attention and begin to establish credibility.

With every trend come three things:
1. Issues that create a challenge for the leader. Issues are obstacles or roadblocks that stand in the leader's path toward the accomplishment of his or her goals, plans, and objectives.
2. With issues come threats—threats that if not addressed can compromise the performance of the leader's organization.
3. With threats the insightful and creative person can see opportunities.

If you were to spend just a couple of hours every week researching the trends, issues, threats, and opportunities that are prevalent in the vertical markets that you focus on and become articulate in your ability to cut to the chase and explain TITO to executives, you will be amazed at how quickly cold introductions will warm up resulting in a meaningful interaction. This is a direct result of the fact that executives are constantly looking for insight and you are clearly demonstrating you have what they want and, frankly, need.

TITO is also very powerful in dealing with receptionists and executive assistants who artfully play the role of gatekeeper. I have found over the years that I will be directed to the people and departments the gatekeeper thinks I am aligned with. If I call a company and I'm asked by the receptionist or an executive assistant, "What is the purpose of your call?" And I respond with, "I sell phone systems." I will be immediately directed to a lower level "technical screener" or worst yet the "purchasing department." On the other hand, if I answer this same question with a TITO related response such as, "I'm calling to speak to Mr. Jones regarding three trends that are currently prevalent in your industry that are having a direct impact on corporate revenues," my chance of getting on Mr. Jones's calendar just increased significantly.

Wright

What role does the "human element" play in today's results-oriented business world?

Cashin

The human element is slowly being drained out of business dealings today. Evidence of this trend is the fact that 85 percent of buyers said they would opt to remove salespeople from transactions. This means we as salespeople are not delivering value in the eyes of the buyer. In order for us to deliver value, not only do we have to have an understanding of TITO we have to be skillful in articulating our insights to our prospect, and that requires the human touch.

The other day I went into my bank, which is a small community bank that I've been doing business with for eighteen years. The tellers and branch manager all know me by name. One of the tellers was helping me make a deposit and she asked, "Duane, you have an ATM card don't you?"

"Yes I do," I replied.

"Did you know that you could have made this deposit right outside at the ATM and you wouldn't have had to come into the bank?"

"Wow, I didn't really realize that." When I walked out of the bank I asked myself: if I were the president of that bank, would I want my tellers explaining to my customers that it's not necessary for them to interface with any bank representatives to do their banking? I realize that the teller was just trying to make my life easier; but in my opinion, suggesting that I do my banking at the ATM is a critical mistake. The desire to make my life easier is not the mistake—it's how they're attempting to go about it that presents the strategic error. The banking industry is just one of many that are very crowded and struggling to create a unique advantage. Will banks be successful in creating an uncommon offer by suggesting we do our banking at an ATM, never talking with a human?

You can also go into a big box store today and purchase a product without talking with a soul. You can find the product you're looking for on the shelf and check yourself out. Is this going to present this company as unique? It's doubtful. The ability to use an automated check-out system is a technology-based option that is easily replicated by any retail organization. More and more we are communicating through e-mail and less and less we find ourselves picking up the phone in an effort to make a personal connection. It is very difficult to differentiate yourself at arm's length. Technology is fantastic and is very helpful in supporting your business growth. However, it is dangerous to think that as a long-term strategy it will be effective in distinguishing your organization from your competition.

Wright

People who have seen you speak have coined the phrase, "The passion of Cashin!" Why is that?

Cashin

When I speak I do get fired up. We're here for a very short time. I'm going to do what is meaningful to me and I'm going to do it with passion. I'm going to spend the rest of my life doing what matters to me while simultaneously helping others.

Some people will argue that what they really want to do will not generate enough money for them to live on. And they will argue that it's not realistic to expect that they can be a success at it. I would argue it's very dangerous not to do what you love for several reasons. If you're not fired up about what you're doing someone else will be and eventually you'll lose your job. And I think it's safe to say that if you're not doing what is meaningful to you then it *is* just a "job." I also suggest that we do not go through our lives striving to be "adequate" at something that is not meaningful to us. There's no juice in "adequate"!

About the Author

After thirteen years of business success in companies ranging in size from medium to Fortune 500 and positions from straight commission salesman to Vice President of Sales, Duane Cashin decided to start his own company. Within four years Duane's grand format graphics company grew to be a multi-million-dollar organization with its work displayed at the Super Bowl, Rockefeller Center, Radio City Music Hall, and MTV's studios at Times Square.

Duane's speaking skills were honed when he joined Tony Parinello, author of *Selling to VITO*. Duane sold and delivered these famous seminars throughout the United States while establishing a sales record still unbroken.

Duane Cashin
P.O. Box 21
North Granby, CT 06060
Phone: 860.916.7081
E-mail: duane@duanecashin.com

Chapter Six

An interview with . . .

John Gray

David Wright (Wright)

John, you've built a successful career as an expert giving relationship advice. I recently read a statement attributed to you: "A wise woman is careful not to pursue a man more than he is pursuing her." Will you explain why?

John Gray (Gray)

When women make themselves too available to men, men get lazy. It's old-fashioned wisdom, but on a new level. We can understand it biochemically as well. Men bond with women when their testosterone levels go up. When there's a challenge, testosterone levels go up. But when things become easy, testosterone levels go down—so there needs to be a sense of the man initiating his own behaviors as to a woman doing it all.

The easiest way to make a man lose interest in you is to do everything for him. The most exciting thing to a man is when he feels that he is making a difference in a woman's life, as opposed to her doing everything for him.

Wright

That makes sense. Perhaps definitions were different several years ago when I was single. Today, how does one determine if he or she is dating or in a "relationship"?

Gray

Quite often women believe that when they are having sex with a man that they are having a monogamous relationship with him. They just assume that is his value system, and that's not always the case. I encourage women to assume that they're having a committed, monogamous relationship after a man has told them so.

The next question that comes up from women is, "Well, how do you bring up such a subject?" The best way to do it is to let him know at some point that you're not interested in having sex unless you're in an exclusive monogamous relationship. When he's ready to make that step she should tell him how she feels about it. That is certainly one approach.

Wright

If someone is not sure that the person he or she is dating is "the one," how can that person get some help to sort through that uncertainty?

Gray

Certainly feeling uncertain and doubting is a natural course of action in the dating process, and it's the first realization that's important. Sometimes people think, "If I don't know for sure, then maybe this is definitely not the right person for me."

One insight that is very important is that you could be with the right person for you, but still go through a period of feeling doubt and uncertainty. It's just a natural process, and while you are in that process it takes time before a part of you begins to sense that you're with the right person, or you begin to sense that you're with the wrong person. It just takes some time.

Couples who rush into making a commitment often make a mistake, and then feelings get hurt, so it's best to go slow when in doubt and not to assume that something's wrong.

Wright

In the event of a cheating spouse or a lover, what should people do to learn to heal from infidelity in the relationship?

Gray

It's an important concept to recognize that we all get our hearts broken, our partners make mistakes, and we experience disappointments. A part of growing in real love is the ability to forgive our partners for mistakes. People simply don't think sometimes and they make mistakes. By talking about it and sharing, people can understand what their mistakes are and make changes and grow from that. It's certainly a personal choice that some people make to simply exclude somebody who would ever cheat on them.

If someone has children I always encourage them to recognize that having an affair is a mistake, and people make mistakes—it's not a horrible, horrible mistake, it's just a mistake.

If someone's violent (that's more of a horrible, horrible mistake), even then it's forgivable if the person was to get help and recognize that he (or she) has a problem and overcome that problem.

The main question about being with someone is that after you have opened your heart and you've been hurt, if you take time to heal your heart, do you still want to be with him or her? That's the question. It's not for me or any other person to tell you whether you should be with that person; it's always an individual choice within the heart. The problem is that some people get caught up in this thinking that if someone makes a mistake then for sure I don't want to be with them. It's quite unrealistic to ever expect perfection in this world.

Wright

In your writings you suggest using a relationship advisor or coach for those who need help. Will you explain the process?

Gray

The process is simply talking with somebody who will ask you questions to help you to get in touch with your feelings. You can express your feelings without feeling that you're going to be judged or your feelings are going to hurt somebody or you're going to be held accountable and stand by those feelings. Often feelings need some room to flow and change as you grow in awareness. It's often not safe to show this with someone you're in a relationship with—the person might hold you to those feelings. So you go to a counselor to talk about those things.

Today it's becoming very popular to talk to coaches as well. One of the differences between a counselor and a coach is that a counselor is trained more academically in the process of analyzing what dysfunction you might have, and in providing a means to reflect on what's happening in your life related to things in your past. The counselor might even do more work on your childhood to rebuild self-esteem issues.

A coach is someone who is there to hold you accountable to do the things that you say you want to do by asking you questions. A coach can also become a sounding board who will ask you about what your feelings are, what happened, what you think should happen, what you think should not have happened, and what you think can happen. This type of exploration helps people find within themselves the wisdom to make better choices in their life. It also helps to motivate them to make better choices and follow up with action. So the coach tends to be more practically oriented.

A Mars/Venus coach adds to it an aspect of providing education as to the various insights of how men and women are different, how their emotional needs are different, and how they can motivate each other to be the best they can be in a relationship, rather than unknowingly pulling out the worst about the individuals in a relationship. I'm a big believer in education first, and then in coaching to motivate people. But often people don't even know what's going on, and some basic insights can help them make better choices and decisions. A coach can then assist them in staying motivated to achieve that end.

Wright

I've heard the divorce rate is 50 percent. Is that true? And can a counselor or relationship coach actually help save a marriage?

Gray

I've seen counselors ruin marriages, and I've seen counselors help save marriages. There are different forms of therapy. If you're in therapy and it doesn't feel right to you and you don't feel like you're making progress, you're probably in the wrong kind of therapy for you. There are some kinds of therapy where the opportunity is created for two people to sit and talk about how they feel with each other. This can result in arguments and fights in the counseling room just like the fights they have at home.

My Mars/Venus counselors are trained in ways to assist individuals in learning new ways of interacting, new ways of expressing their feelings, and new ways of avoiding arguments and fights. I think this is very important for a therapist to do. A Mars/Venus coach is going to focus more on assisting individuals in taking responsibility for how they're contributing to the problems in their relationship. This can simply be having someone to talk with to share what you're feeling. Sharing your feelings can sometimes bring about enormous insight into a situation, as well as helping you to feel better.

When you feel better you're able to respond in a more positive way. Our Mars/Venus coaches and counselors repeatedly receive stories and testimonials of couples who feel that their marriages were saved.

Wright

I went on your Web site and I looked at some of the things that you're doing. I was really impressed. One thing that caught my eye was the Relationship Test. Does the Mars/Venus Relationship Test really work? What do you actually test?

Gray

There are different areas of relationships which could be stronger or weaker. What a Relationship Test does is allows you to become more aware of what you're experiencing every day. Often people do not take the time to sit down and reflect on what's working here and what's not working. Our lives are often so busy that we're just going from the *next* thing to the *next* thing to the *next* thing, and we don't sit back and reflect on what's working and what's not working.

By doing the test and answering the questions, you're having to take that time and reflect upon what really is going on in your relationship. The irony in relationships is sometimes couples will be fighting in counseling or they'll be fighting at home, and they don't even know what they are fighting about. They don't even know how the argument started! Everything was fine, and suddenly one little thing happens and one or the other is flying off the handle and they just don't know what to do about it.

Often these flying off the handle experiences are like the water boiling and turning into steam. Long before it boiled, it simmered, and long before it simmered, the water was heating up. So there's a process that leads up to uncontrolled experiences in relationships. When you become more aware of what's not working in a relationship long before it's boiling, you have a chance to easily make adjustments in your behavior.

When taking a Relationship Test you're able to see many places where you have confusion or you don't understand what is going on. Talking to a relationship coach you can ask questions, particularly in the problem areas. You can talk about what's going on so that you can make sense of what's going on in your relationship.

Often when we don't know what's happening or don't know how to correctly interpret what's happening because it doesn't make sense to us, we then assume the worst rather than assume the best. And what our Mars/Venus coaches do is help to point out the *good* reasons why people do what they do, and strategies to help bring out the best in them.

Wright

Every time I hear a talk show host ask a guest about the most important attribute a person needs to have when considering a relationship, the answer from males or females are always the same: "A good sense of humor." Is that really true?

Gray

Well, that's what everybody says, but when difficulties arise in relationships the women then complain that the men are not serious. Or the man could complain that the woman isn't serious. Generally it's the number one thing on the list for women to say "a man's sense of humor," and when I hear that I want then to educate that woman to recognize that she's looking for the wrong thing. The last thing you need is for a man to entertain you. What you want is a man to provide security for you, to be attentive to you, and to understand you. In that place of safety, then you will naturally be expressive of your femininity, which is actually quite entertaining to men. It's the woman who brings joy to life, not the man. So when women are looking for men to bring joy to their life, women are often just feeling insecure as though they can't provide enough, and they are looking to a man to provide that role.

I have a wife and three daughters. When I travel with them it's amazing how entertaining they are! The nature of femininity is that women talk, they share, they look, they comment, they respond, they laugh a lot.

But what *is* good for a woman to look for in a man is not entertainment. She may think she's looking for that, but she'll find herself being disappointed again and again. What she should be looking for is a man's sense of humor in that he doesn't take things too seriously. That's extremely very attractive to women. Not taking himself too seriously means that he's not defensive about things and he doesn't claim to be perfect or expect or demand that she believes him to be perfect. That is a very healthy attitude and attribute in a man. If he can, in a sense, "lighten up," that constitutes a good sense of humor. That is what creates a sense of security for a woman.

If women want men to entertain them all the time, not only will they be disappointed, but it puts way too much pressure on men—they'll come on really strong and then women will lose interest because men are just not entertainers.

Wright

Is it possible to be too cautious setting your criteria too high when choosing a life partner?

Gray

I think the idea that you are getting at is very healthy to examine. I hesitate to say, "Lower your expectations and find your ideal partner." That sounds like you're not getting the best. What is going on today with both women and men is that they have very unrealistic expectations of what they require and what they want in a partner.

Life is often a gradual process of humbling them and helping them recognize what's realistic and what they are really looking for. We often look to the cover of a book rather than to the substance of the book, hence the old saying, "Don't judge a book by its cover." In our society we have become somewhat superficial in how we look for people. It takes a little maturing before we begin to realize who a person is is much more than how they look or how they react in certain situations or what they have or what they can do.

And yet those are all a part of the picture. I focus on helping couples change their expectations just in a sense of what a healthy relationship looks like. It doesn't mean that he's being romantic all the time, and it doesn't mean that she's happy all the time—two people really need to learn how to be happy on their own and then want to share that happiness with someone. That becomes the foundation of a relationship. When we are looking to someone to fill us up and make us happy, we will be disappointed later on. When we are somewhat happy and fulfilled in our own life, then we can find extra happiness through sharing our happiness with someone else. When that happens we are much less needy and our expectations tend to be much more realistic automatically.

Wright

Almost everything you've said has hit me personally, especially the aspect of education. You see people who say, "This is my life-long partner" and they talk about all kinds of things, but it seems like you're talking about education.

Gray

I feel that what's missing most in the world today when it comes to relationships is insight and education into understanding how to create healthy relationships. And why we need this education now more so than a hundred years ago, is that people didn't take courses even fifty years ago in improving their relationships. That's because there were hundreds of years of tradition where women had certain roles and men had certain roles. Men interacted in certain ways and women interacted in certain ways. As long as everybody acted according to those established patterns, everyone got along quite well.

Then the world changed. Now the world is different and yet no one has defined new roles and how men and women are supposed to interact and what works best for them. To a certain extent there is no "best"—it's a world of tremendous freedom and choice and we have to define those roles ourselves. But in defining those roles there's a certain amount of freedom to create those roles, and there's also a certain lack of freedom.

I might wish to walk through a wall, but I just can't—certain realities don't change. So in this world where we are "making up" relationships in a new way, there are certain realities that have not changed. There are certain ways that men interact and there are certain ways that women interact. There are certain needs that women have and certain needs that men have. The needs men and women have are different. By understanding those differences we can then realistically work with those differences to support each other better at this time of enormous change and enormous stress in our lives due to that change.

And what is interesting is that men and women react differently to stress, so most of the differences that cause frustration between men and women are simply differences that we don't understand, and those differences that we don't instinctively relate to are particularly how men and women react to stress.

For example, men will often become quiet or distant under stress, whereas women will want to open up and share and talk under stress. And then, taking another step that stresses even more, women will then *not* want to talk because they'll feel that they've tried to talk and no one listened so they begin to close up, and then they have no way to effectively cope with stress.

On the other hand, you've got men who tend to naturally pull away and mull things over to feel better under stress. If they are really under a huge amount of stress, these men don't even take the time to pull away. They go into a more talkative mode—they just want to complain and point out how they are victims in life. This becomes very distressing to women, and they go further and further away. That's what I would call "role reversal," which is another problem occurring today.

There are a lot of combinations in men and women and we just don't understand how to make sense of it, but by having a basic understanding of how men and women are different and how they cope with stress differently, we can then be better equipped to support our partners when they are under a lot of stress.

For example, if my wife doesn't want to talk about something, I can be helpful to her and be cooperative, which will lower her stress level. She will then begin to open up and talk, which will lower her stress level even more—as long as I make it safe for her to talk.

If a man is stressed and is complaining a lot and talking a lot, then what a woman can do is instead of trying to be a good listener, she can simply ask him to talk with his friends and give her some room to do what she wants to do. She should not encourage him to talk about all the things that are going wrong in his life. As she leaves him alone he will then be able to cope with stress better. He will then "come out of his cave" so to speak and be much more friendly to her. Women have to recognize that when men are in a bad mood or when they're stressed out, it's not up to her to do anything for him. Men have to come out of this primarily on their own, otherwise they tend to become weak.

So these are primary differences that a woman wouldn't think of. Another example is if a woman's feeling stressed out and he comes to her and asks her questions to help open her up and give her support, it will actually empower her. And doing so empowers the man. But when a woman is too much like a mother to a man, it will weaken him and she will resent it later as well, that's a no-win situation.

Wright

I have known you for several years and I have always been impressed by your ability to stay on the leading edge of the subjects you are passionate about. Have you found any new information about relationship-building in the past few of years that might help people make fewer mistakes in the search for love and companionship?

Gray

I think that in a sense I was touching on that a few minutes ago when I mentioned the subject of stress. Stress has become so high that not only do men and women have strong stress reactions, they actually go further into a role reversal where women are so stressed that they feel they have to do everything themselves and they become very much like a man. Men become so stressed that they begin to complain about their lives and feel like they're not responsible for their lives anymore. This is the wrong direction, and yet it's a natural stress reaction.

Today we are experiencing unprecedented amounts of stress with longer commuting hours and higher costs of living, balancing work and home life, increased information, and cell phones, talking, and being connected to work all the time. All this is putting a huge new burden on our lives and on our relationships.

What I have done is help to point this out, which can help couples enormously. Couples can recognize that there are ways to lower stress. If we are going to have more dramatic stress, there are more dramatic ways that couples can lower the stress levels for each other. Those ways happen to be women learning to ask for help—that's a real big issue—and men being more responsive to give help. That's not to say they have to do it every time she asks as if he's supposed to "jump to it." There are times when you are supposed to take your rest, so there needs to be understanding of that.

Women often resent having to ask for help, and that is something that has to change. She has to recognize that when you grow up in this world you have to learn how to ask for things, particularly in the business world. Likewise in relationships, if a woman wants her partner to change his natural mode of behavior she needs to *ask*. She shouldn't expect him to be like a woman who would just tend to think about everything that needs to be done until overwhelmed doing it—men typically don't fall into that role. So she needs to ask him, and when people ask others to do something, when they do it they need to let them know it's appreciated.

This is a new skill for a woman. While women sometimes resist this, once they practice it they realize, "Wow, this isn't that hard, and it works!" So that's one way to lower stress in life—if women are not feeling supported to *ask* for it in a way that will work rather than the way that they do ask, which often doesn't work. Practice "realistic expectations." Instead of complaining that "I can't walk through this wall" and "Why doesn't the wall open up for me?" you've got to find the door and learn how to open it!

The second important area to lower stress is in the realm of communication. Women want more sharing and more communication and men aren't providing that. There's a way that men can provide it—if women cooperate. As I said before, women should ask for what they want. Maybe a woman could say something like, "I'd like for you to listen to what is going on in my life." Let him know that he doesn't have to say anything. In fact, I encourage that in the beginning—he should say nothing, and let her talk for five or ten minutes. She then thanks him for listening, and then walks away. While this seems very unnatural, it is a super stress reducer once people start to experience it. It's quite amazing.

I didn't invent this—this is what has been going on for years in the therapy office. Women come in and they talk about what's going on in their lives and they feel better. The therapist doesn't say much at all. And the better the therapist, the less the therapist says and the more questions the therapist asks.

So the secret here is learning how to talk about what is bothering you without expecting a solution or without expecting your partner to "fix" you or fix the situation in some way. So she can set up that conversation and she will feel better; he'll feel better too because he helped her. And men like helping their wives.

The third area is romance. Again, in this area couples stopped having romance, and romance is actually one of the most strong and powerful stress reducers. It's just that when we're under stress the last thing we think about is romance, both for her and for him. Yet the difference is women will often think about how much they miss it. They're not necessarily feeling romantic, but they often complain that "he's not romantic," implying that she wants him to be romantic so she can feel good again. I understand that and I respect that. And I have a solution for that, but it's not waiting for him—you have to ask! Now, what woman would ever think to ask for romance? Well *you* can. It's a very simple thing.

To solve this problem women have to learn how to ask, and men have to learn how to respond. Women then have to learn how to appreciate that, and the solutions do occur. Women can't expect a man to be a mind-reader. He doesn't know what's going on inside her head and in her heart. Asking for romance is something so foreign that women need a few examples of it and then they can get the hang of it.

For example, she shouldn't say, "You're not romantic, we don't experience romance anymore, we never go out anymore, we're not having fun anymore." Those are just negative complaints. Instead she needs to focus more on what's positive. For example, "Hey, this particular band is playing in town this weekend. Would you get tickets for the concert?" The woman asks the man—that's it. It's a very simple thing. The woman could say, "Oh, we haven't gone out this week, would you get tickets for this or that?" or simply, "Would you pick a movie and we'll go see the movies?" or "Would you make reservations and let's go out to eat?" The man could say, "Where would you like to go?" The woman could say, "Whatever you want to pick."

Women can start defining romance as letting him decide where to go, her asking for it, him deciding, and her having a good time just being with him! And gradually that moves into more discretion about what you're going to do and so forth. This process will begin to restore the woman's confidence in the man. All the woman needs to do is to just ask and let him know that whatever he does will be fine.

Just as it was in the beginning when he was so romantic, men often become unromantic because they try, but after a while women start picking out what he did wrong. And men will think, "Well she's so picky I'll just let her decide." And that's the end of romance because part of what reduces stress for women is that she does not have to decide. And when a woman comes back to the realization that having the man make some decisions and she doesn't have to decide will actually lower her stress enormously. It also lowers a man's stress enormously when he knows that whatever he decides she's going to like, as opposed to feeling that he's going to put his best out thee and she's going to step all over it by pointing out what he did wrong. She doesn't mean to do that, but that's the net effect.

So these are extra additions, extra awarenesses, and insights that can help couples to cope with the extra stress they're experiencing in their lives today.

Wright

If you had to "bottom line" the reasons for the success of your Mars and Venus books, products, ideas, and counseling help, what would the main reason be?

Gray

I think that because the world has changed, people are eager and hungry to have a new way of understanding the world in a positive light. When we don't understand what is going on around us, we just assume something's wrong. By learning the new insights regarding how men and women are different, and how we look at the world differently in a *positive* way, they are released from having to blame their partners or blame themselves. They are motivated to find creative solutions that make their relationships better. So in one aspect, what I do is give people permission to make mistakes, and give them insight to solve the problems.

Wright

An interesting conversation! I always learn so much when I talk with you. It's just incredible. I really do appreciate this time that you've spent with me today, and I really think the readers are going to get a lot out of it.

Gray

Well thank you so much. It's a pleasure.

About the Author

Dr. John Gray is the author of fifteen books, including *Men Are from Mars, Women Are from Venus* (Harper Collins 1992), a number one best-selling relationship book. Over thirty million *Mars and Venus* books have been sold in over forty languages throughout the world.

Dr. John Gray, a certified family therapist, is the premier Better Life relationship coach on AOL. In 2001, he received the Smart Marriages Impact Award. John Gray received his degree in 1982 from Columbia Pacific University. He has authored fourteen other best-selling books. His book, *The Mars & Venus Diet & Exercise Solution* (St. Martin's Press 2003), reveals why diet, exercise, and communication skills combine to effect the production of healthy brain chemicals and how the need for those chemicals differ between men and women.

An internationally recognized expert in the fields of communication and relationships, Dr. Gray's unique focus is assisting men and women in understanding, respecting, and appreciating their differences. For decades, he has conducted public and private seminars for thousands of participants. In his highly acclaimed books, audiotapes, and videotapes, as well as in his seminars, Dr. Gray entertains and inspires audiences with his practical insights and easy to use communication techniques that can be immediately applied to enrich relationships and quality of life.

Dr. Gray is a popular speaker on the national and international lecture circuit and often appears on television and radio programs to discuss his work. He has made guest appearances on such shows as Oprah, Good Morning America, The Today Show, The CBS Morning Show, Live with Regis, The View, Politically Incorrect, Larry King Live, The Roseanne Show, CNN and Company, and many others. He has been profiled in USA Today, Newsweek, TIME Magazine, TV Guide, People, Forbes, and numerous other major publications across the United States.

Dr. Gray's nationally syndicated column reaches millions of readers in many newspapers, including The Atlanta Journal/Constitution, New York Daily News, New York Newsday, The Denver Post, and the San Antonio Express-News. Internationally, the columns appear in publications in England, Canada, Mexico, Korea, Latin America, and the South Pacific.

Dr. Gray lives with his wife and three children in Northern California.

John Gray
www.askmarsvenus.com

Chapter Seven

An interview with . . .

Chuck McCants

David Wright (Wright)

Today we are talking with Chuck McCants. Chuck is a veteran of the Hospitality and Advertising Industries and a Licensed Florida Real Estate Professional. As vice president of Barnhills Buffet from 2000 to 2005, Chuck led dozens of new store openings. He trained hundreds of unit employees and managers, developed key corporate leaders, and helped develop a team of 2,500 associates who produced sales revenues of 100 million plus. He understands the demands of the business manager and that of corporate leadership.

Chuck shares his beliefs on how to manage the opportunities of daily operations and achieve the rewards that exceptional management and leadership present. As Sales Manager at America's Top Realty, Inc. in Gulf Breeze, Florida, Chuck says, "Regardless of the industry you are in, living with a selfless and 'living-to-win' attitude and mindset is a sure way to reach the pinnacles of success you have set for you and your team."

Chuck, welcome to *Conversations on Success.*

Chuck McCants (McCants)

Thank you David; I'm glad to be here.

Wright

How do you define success in your life and in the lives of others?

McCants

I believe that the definition of success is unique and different to each individual. What I am saying is that each person defines his or her own level of success. For me success is achieving the things in life that bring happiness and fulfillment to me and my family. I also believe that there are different definitions and levels of success at different times and at different ages in life. Again, all the definitions of success are unique at that time and to every individual. A team might define success as achieving a certain sports award or academic achievement. As you graduate college, success is achieving that perfect job, relationship, or lifestyle. As you season a little bit and move into your forties and fifties, success may be summed up as simply a quality of life, balance, and financial stability. Sometimes we find ourselves starting all over again with new careers, new relationships, and new dreams. As you redefine success you establish new goals and dreams.

Wright

What would you say would be the biggest contribution to your professional success?

McCants

I think the biggest contribution to my success is clearly determination to get the job or project done. It simply drives me crazy to be late on a deadline. I always strive to complete a project ahead of time. I have never liked having people look over my shoulders or push me in order to get what they have asked for. In addition to that, I have a strong determination to help others achieve the things they want in life in the process.

Wright

Aside from personal role models, who are the people who have served as your role models for success?

McCants

The obvious role models are God and my parents. God has always provided for me and I honor Him in all that I do. My mother was a great southern cook and a fanatic about cleanliness. I think that is where I learned my love for cooking and my attention to detail.

My grandmother played a large part in shaping and molding the person that I have become. In addition to being a great southern cook (man, could she make biscuits!), she was a very determined lady. Even until her death, which was preceded with Alzheimer's and Parkinson's, she would work from dawn to dusk. She loved to till the soil.

My father taught me the meaning of a good work ethic. He was a sales manager with Liberty National Life Insurance Company for over thirty years. He would start before seven in the morning and finish the day somewhere around in nine at night. He was a giving and caring man and a great provider for his family.

Another person who has contributed to my success is my close friend, Skip Martin, who lives in Atlanta. He is a genius when it comes to entrepreneurial development. He has run multiple companies and is on his way to being a multi-millionaire today. He has a drive that won't stop. I think the drive he has in his personal, family, and business life really makes a difference.

Another individual, Steve Barnhill, founder of the family buffet chain Barnhill's, is truly a symbol of perseverance. Here is a guy at who at nineteen years old was washing dishes in his father's restaurant and thirty years later is president and CEO of a major chain. Steve has determination and the desire to succeed! All of these individuals have been mentors to me.

Wright

What do you think are the biggest obstacles people face in trying to become successful?

McCants

I think lack of clarity about what will make a person happy is the key to why many people fail in their efforts to succeed. Many people believe that money is the key to happiness and that is most often what we all strive for. This is because we grow up believing that money will bring us true happiness and success. The truth is: money doesn't create happiness. Watch the evening news, read the paper, surf the 'Net and you'll see people you think would be totally happy because they have everything in the world, yet they are the most miserable people in the world. I am often saddened for them because they are missing the simplicity of true success—the belief in oneself, faith, and surrounding yourself with people you can give to as well receive from in life. Those are the things I believe contribute most to one's level of success in life.

Wright

How do you know what to do or what you need to be successful?

McCants

I think the first step is prioritizing your goals. Start with your dreams. Everyone has dreams. If you don't have any dreams today take a moment, close your eyes, and dream right this minute! Now write down what you dreamed of and start pursuing that dream. Prioritize, write down your dreams. Create a plan to achieve them. Zig Ziglar and the best of the best tell you to write your goals down—put your goals on paper and prioritize!

Life can be confusing and challenging. Rewards in life are not handed to most people. Rewards have to be worked for and earned. It is easy to be distracted, but having your priorities in order will help you clarify your goals.

When you have prioritized your goals you can then better define them. Define, execute, and achieve. Dream *big!* As you define, execute, and achieve your goals it will become easier for you to achieve the bigger goals you dream of.

Wright

Would you tell our readers a little bit about what drives you to be successful?

McCants

It is clearly my family, serving God, and serving others. I really am a servant leader. That is my management style. Although I want to be successful and I have my personal goals, my personal goals are always inclusive of others achieving their goals. I get tremendous satisfaction from seeing others achieve success. I have been fortunate enough to achieve personal success in the process of helping others. You can do that at any level whether you are a retail manager, construction worker, or an executive in a company. If you just help others get the things in life they want, then ultimately you will get the things in life you want.

Wright

Is it important to have balance in your life to be successful and if it is, how do you balance your success with your life?

McCants

Obviously the answer is yes. I think that once you've achieved the success you desire in life you have to evaluate where you are in that success. You need to do this along the way as well. When doing this you will discover you have achieved benchmarks and levels of success almost without even being aware of it. You are in the process of working toward that goal then all of a sudden you've accomplished it. Check in with life. Evaluate where you are in life, with your family, and with God.

During the ten years when I was traveling with Barnhill's Buffet, visiting our stores, helping to motivate our managers and crew members, and promoting our brand, it was easy to just work. At the time I traveled for Barnhill's we had as many as fifty restaurants at one time; I was on the road about forty weeks a year. When you work 24/7 it is easy to move apart from God, family, and friends. It is important to check in and find out where your relationships are. Discover if you are giving enough to your family, your friends, and to God. Are you spending the quality time that you need to spend with your family when you are home? It is difficult at times, but you just have to take that time and look at where you are and do some evaluating. Find that balance and then re-evaluate where you are going.

Wright

So what are the messages you want people to hear so they can learn from your success?

McCants

The basic concept I want others to hear is to be able to give away what you learn. Early in my career as a restaurant manager I managed a restaurant outside of Atlanta. I promoted several of the managers beneath me to general managers within the area. I was a general manager of a restaurant and I would hear managers say, "Why are you giving all of this away? Why are you telling these others how to run a store profitably, how to run a P & L, how to grow profits and sales?"

The reason I promoted these people was that when I wasn't there, my associates—my assistant managers—had the ability, knowledge, and the tools to run that restaurant as effectively as I ran it. So when I went out on a conference or a trip I didn't have to worry about who was taking care of the store. Because of that I had those managers who were promoted, who were successful, and who were grateful for what I was willing to teach and give to them.

I think this is a very basic philosophy. I think that individuals have difficulty with delegating responsibility because they fear for their position—they fear someone else may take their job. The greatest compliment you can have is to have someone successfully promoted while under your leadership. If you are committed to doing things right and teach others the same, then you are going to be promoted in the process.

Wright

You talked about people who influenced your life such as your father and Zig Ziglar. How can people help other people succeed?

McCants

I think there are four areas where people can help others:

Be supportive—whether you are supportive of your children, your brother, sister, or your spouse, it's important to support them and their goals. Support them in their efforts.

Be positive—Lift up people and their goals. Don't be a naysayer. Don't bring them down. Lift them up. Believe with the individual that he or she can achieve the goals set. The best thing you can do is to be supportive, even if you don't understand or don't believe; give people 100 percent support. Truly care for people's efforts.

Give—Give advice; give what you can to help that person succeed.

Lead—Lead the way for people, run for them, open doors, help them get started. Sometimes all a person needs is just a little push or a little pull. A lot of people never get the push or the pull to get out of the gate.

Those are things I believe you can do to help others.

Wright

You speak about passion being our compass for life and that it is a main factor in attaining success. Do you think passion alone is enough?

McCants

Passion is the heart of the engine that moves us forward and that moves us toward our goals. It is passion that moves us to relationships, to career choices, and to achieve our dreams. Passion coupled with a strong positive self-image and clarity of goals creates an unstoppable drive for accomplishment. Passion is the driving force.

Wright

Passion is such a "soft" subject and intangible. Will you define passion for our readers—at least as you see it?

McCants

I think I have already said it. Passion is what gets the job done. It is what moves us toward the goal. Passion can be felt emotionally and is often described as a feeling—an inner yearning to accomplish a goal. Look at Lance Armstrong and the achievements he made in the Tour de France. He didn't do that just because he wanted to ride a bike. He was passionate about what his achievements were going to be. He was passionate about conquering cancer. He was passionate about winning the Tour de France seven consecutive times. It is motivating to see passion demonstrated in that way. Passion is what draws us to athletes, actors, and top performers in all areas of life.

You don't have to be a professional athlete or actress to display your passion. Passion can be demonstrated at any time by anyone. Passion is demonstrated every day by our soldiers in the Middle East, by teachers in the classroom, and by doctors in the emergency room. It is clearly what gets the job done.

Wright

When people follow their passion and excel, does their success produce more passion?

McCants

I think it depends on where you are in life—not necessarily how old you are, but rather, what your circumstances and desires are. Look at Jack LaLanne who in his nineties is still teaching people the basics of nutrition and physical fitness. When you see him in person you think he is in his fifties. What he started at the age of twenty-one against great opposition he continues today with great success!

Success can sometimes silence passion when accomplishment is realized. Depending where you are in life will determine the level of passion and drive you have.

Wright

What makes your perspective unique?

McCants

My perspective is that I believe we all have the opportunity to give more and to achieve more than we realize.

I would like to share a program that I have developed to help individuals do just that. The program is called "Living to Win." "Living to Win" offers the perspective that when you live a life that mirrors the life of Christ, when you walk the walk and approach life with a Christ-like mindset, you are inevitably going to achieve a higher level of fulfillment in life. I truly believe that by doing this, not only will you be more fulfilled personally, but others around you will achieve a higher level of fulfillment as well because they can see the desire and difference that God has placed in you.

Wright

What is "Living to Win"?

McCants

"Living to Win" is a life path—a personal development program based on living a Christ-like walk and maintaining a Christ-like attitude in every step you take, every breath you breathe, and every thought that you have. It is based on a couple of basic principles: prayer and goal-setting. In addition, "Living to Win" requires individuals to seek God in every aspect of life and view life with the vision of God's eyes. If you can just imagine what a difference it would make if we all could look at people and circumstances through the eyes of God and see the positive in every person and every situation.

In "Living to Win" there are nine steps to creating life-changing habits in individuals. These habits listed below will not only change the life of the individual, but will impact the lives of everyone the individual comes into contact with:

Start and end your day with prayer. Prepare for your successes with God by setting aside a time for prayer in the morning and in the evening. It doesn't have to be hours but it does need to be consistent, reverent, and genuine. I believe that God has a place in His heart for your prayers. He wants you to seek His wisdom and direction. The key to prayer is doing it and believing that God will provide answers to your prayer.

Visualize your day and the accomplishments you will make in it. God will show you every step, the people, and the methods. He will take you to the doors of opportunity and open them for you. All you will have to do is execute the process.

Seek God and the good in people and circumstances by using God's vision. Look with the vision of God's eyes to see the positive in every person and every situation. Don't be quick to judge. Be quick to love and understand.

Learn to meet and greet people in the love of Christ. Greet people with enthusiasm in the spirit of God. As your confidence grows and as your faith grows, people will begin to see God's spirit in your eyes, your voice, and your walk.

Maintain a balanced physical life. God wants us to be healthy. Find the time to do the things you need to do to make sure that your body is well tuned.

Feed your mind with positive input. We live in a world of unlimited opportunities and endless possibilities. Strive to achieve your top potential by focusing on what is positive and brings glory to God. Seek His wisdom, direction, and favor. Spend time in God's Word. It is the perfect blueprint for every aspect of life. Grow in your relationship with God and God will grow you.

Take time to be alone. Clear your mind and observe the beauties of God's creation. Life is busy. We are easily distracted by life's activities. Take time to be quiet and be alone.

Spend time with those you love. Take time to be with your family and friends. It is easy to distance yourself from your family. With both parents working full-time jobs in most homes, being able to have dinner together is a challenge. It is easy to pass your kids in the hall and not even have a conversation. To have a healthy family life you need to be able to give and receive emotional support and stimulation. Every person needs a certain level of emotional support. I am talking about being around those you love. Spend dedicated time with those people you care for and love—your family and your friends.

Share what you believe. Share the love that you have for God. Share the love that you have for life. There is someone out there who wants and needs what you have experienced and know to be true. Share and change lives!

Wright

Why is fulfillment different from success?

McCants

As I said earlier, success is different for each individual at different levels in life. Fulfillment is a result of our successes and achievements. Fulfillment is not always success-driven. Fulfillment for many people can be found simply in being able to provide for their family. It can be having a certain relationship, such as a husband and wife. I think there is sadness in some people who never have fulfillment in a relationship or never have the joy of having someone else in their life.

I believe fulfillment is God-given. I believe that God has a plan for every individual. I believe that if you seek Him in everything you do, He will provide an abundant level of fulfillment for you. In that respect, fulfillment is greatly different than success. Although God brings levels of success in life, many people will never reach the level of fulfillment God has planned for them.

Wright

Is someone who has fulfillment seen differently than someone who has great success?

McCants

I think so. Without mentioning names, if you look at the daily headlines you will see some of the most successful people in the world with some of the most troubling situations in life. Clearly they are at a point where they do not have the fulfillment in life they desire. Now I am not speaking for them, but it doesn't seem to me that people who are spending time in rehab or in jail are receiving much fulfillment in their lives by doing so. Although many of these people have reached the pinnacle of success by worldly standards, they are obviously unhappy in their lives.

Several of these are people our children look to as role models—as mentors. Even suicide has been glamorized by this crowd. This is why it is more and more important for parents to take responsibility of raising their children. We can't allow the lives of those we love to fall into the hands of those who don't care or don't have the true love and affection of a loving God. My hope is that there will be individuals who become successful and who at the same time have great faith, discipline, and fulfillment in their lives so they are able to share that with the public. This way the public's view of success will not be driven by individuals who live lives out of balance, but who live lives that are stable and balanced.

Wright

Does living a Christ-like life, as you have referred to it, lead to success?

McCants

I don't think that it leads to success in the terms a majority of people would define as success. I do believe it leads to a life of fulfillment, which can be viewed as being more important than success. I think that if you truly are living a Christ-like life and you have a Christ-like attitude, if you are walking a Christ-like walk and you are sharing that love and joy with everyone you come in contact with, I think it is pretty hard not to become successful or reach the level of success in life that you are striving for. I believe God opens doors for those who Love Him and honor Him.

Wright

What a great conversation. I really appreciate the time you've spent with me to answer these questions. There have been some important answers and I have learned a lot here today. I'm sure that our readers will also.

McCants

Thank you. I appreciate the time and my hope is that those who read will be able to take away some level of meaning out of this chapter and out of our conversation that can change their life or change the life of someone they know. I truly believe we are here on this earth to make a difference in the lives of others. I hope those who read this book will take that to heart and go out and make a difference in someone's life.

Wright

Today we've been talking with Chuck McCants. As an author, speaker, and trainer Chuck shares his beliefs on how to manage the opportunities of daily operations and achieve the rewards that exceptional management and leadership present. As sales manager of America's Top Reality, Inc. in Gulf Breeze, Florida, Chuck says that regardless of the industry you are in, leading with a selfless and living-to-win attitude and mindset is a sure way to reach the pinnacle of success you have set for yourself and your team.

Chuck, thank you so much for being with us on *Conversations on Success*.

About the Author

Chuck McCants is a veteran of the restaurant, advertising, and Real Estate industries. As Vice President of Operations, Chuck helped to develop the southeastern family dining chain known as Barnhill's Buffet. Over the ten years spent with Barnhill's, Chuck lead over thirty new store openings, trained hundreds of unit employees and managers, developed key corporate leaders, and lead a team of 2,500 to produce revenues of $100 million plus.

Chuck understands the demands of the unit manager and that of corporate leadership. Chuck shares his beliefs on how to manage the opportunities of daily operations and achieve the rewards that exceptional management and leadership bring!

Chuck's specialty is delivering "Living to Win, a personal development program that guides people to find the fulfillment in life God has planned for them.

"Living to Win" emphasizes the importance of having a Christ-like attitude and walk in our daily lives and the impact doing so can have on oneself and others.

Topics covered include Positive Self Image, Life Balance, Goal-setting, Motivation, and Relationships.

Chuck's Speaking Topics include: "Living To Win, 9 Steps to attaining a 'Living-to-Win' attitude!," "Discovering Your 'Living-to-Win' Qualities and Talents!," "Delivering the 'Service' in Great Customer Service," "Positive Sales Start with YOU!," and "Goals Accomplished!"

Chuck McCants
Author, Speaker, and Trainer
1221 Northbrook Drive
Pensacola, FL 32504
Phone: 850.712.9077
E-mail: Chuck@livetowin.com
www.livetowin.com

Chapter Eight

An interview with . . .

Bruce Carter

David Wright (Wright)

Today we are talking with Bruce Carter, founder and president of North American Fire Sales. Bruce is a sales trainer and motivational speaker specializing in the fire protection and life safety industry.

In demand throughout both the United States and Canada and with a style that is uniquely his own, Bruce delivers an inspiring message that is down-to-earth yet powerfully hard-hitting. Addressing more than one hundred audiences annually, his keynote presentations, public seminars, and in-house sales workshops educate and inspire while challenging audiences to do and be their best every day.

A recognized sales authority and contributor in print as well, Bruce's high content articles on the selling profession have been featured favorites in scores of publications both in and out of the fire protection arena.

Bruce, welcome to *Conversations on Success*.

Bruce Carter (Carter)

Thank you, David. It is a pleasure being here.

Wright

Well, not to put you on the spot the very first thing Bruce, but I have got to ask, is what I read about you true—at one time you actually rode bulls in professional rodeo?

Carter

David, I'm not sure if I'm proud say, excited to share, or actually a bit reluctant to admit it, but yes, I was an official, dues-paying, card-holding, dust-stirring member of the Rodeo Cowboys Association back in the early seventies and bull-riding was my event.

Wright

I must admit, I have interviewed a number of people who have become successful via some rather unconventional routes, but riding on the back of a 2000 pound Brahma bull has not been one of the more common ones.

Carter

I am not a bit surprised about that. Being from Texas, bull-riding must have been in my blood from the beginning. As a boy, I spent time with a great uncle who was a retired cowboy and someone I looked up to a great deal. It was my uncle Russell who got me involved in professional rodeo and who my mother admitted years later that she wanted to choke! I loved the thrill of the sport and the life of a rodeo cowboy, but after countless stitches, scrapes, and broken bones, I eventually came to the realization that there were probably quite a few career options that would be less hazardous to my health.

Wright

Bruce, now that the dust of the rodeo arena has settled, and as a successful sales professional, trainer, and speaker, how do you define success?

Carter

Success is most certainly defined differently by different people I'm sure, but I believe it must be at least partially defined as the formation and achievement of worthwhile goals. It is the composition and formation of those worthwhile goals in life that is without a doubt the most challenging step in the journey to success for many people.

The person fortunate enough to have a clearly defined mental picture of precisely what he or she wants to do, become, and have in life is a blessed individual indeed. Many of us have known people who, almost from early childhood, seemed to know precisely what they wanted to do with their lives. In many cases we watched them work with a focused ambition and drive until they eventually achieved exactly what they set out to do.

On the other hand, we know folks who, as Zig Ziglar would say, seem to simply remain "wandering generalities" instead of becoming "meaningful specifics." They never discover their true purpose or passion in life. Success for these people remains understandably elusive. Sadly, they seem to flounder in mediocrity for, well, a lifetime in some cases.

Once a person has decided upon a set of worthwhile goals, the early stages of the achievement phase can actually be much easier. As the late Dr. Maxwell Maltz revealed in his classic self-help book, *Psycho-Cybernetics,* all human beings come equipped with an amazing, goal-seeking servo-mechanism already installed within. That mechanism, placed inside each of us by the Master Himself, is directed toward the target with the aid of our own self-image. A healthy and positive self-image steers us toward a life of success, achievement, and happiness while a negative picture of self can point us toward an unfulfilled life of failure and discontent.

Wright

Were Dr. Maltz's observations about the role and importance of the self-image the forerunner of the term we know today as *visualization*?

Carter

Yes, exactly. The overwhelming majority of today's professional athletes understand firsthand the exciting benefits of clearly visualizing the winning outcome of the play, the game, or the entire athletic season. Tiger Woods mentally "sees" the thirty-foot putt dropping into the cup long before he actually attempts the shot on the golf course. Michael Jordan would clearly picture his exciting three-point shots swishing through the net hundreds of times in his own mind's eye well in advance of the actual playoff series.

Interestingly, in 1972, a mentor of mine in the rodeo game was a five-foot seven, 135-pound bull rider by the name of Gary Leffew. Gary told of the many days and nights he would spend alone in the hill country around his home in Santa Maria, California, clearly visualizing his success in professional sports' most dangerous event. He described that, while spending time alone in those California hills, he would visualize himself time after time riding the most cantankerous Brahma bulls to win not only the big jackpot prize money but the world championship. He said, "After seeing myself ride those bulls like a world champion so many times in my mind, my mind didn't know the difference. I came out of those hills walking, talking, and riding like a true champion." In 1970, Gary Leffew was crowned professional rodeo's World Champion Bull Rider!

In our *Sell To Win* and *Fire It Up!* seminars, I spend quite a bit of time discussing the vital importance of not only setting well-defined goals in the selling field but also clearly visualizing the positive outcome of each and every sales call.

As a working sales manager for many years I was often amused at how some struggling salespeople claimed they could simply look at the outside of a particular building and know with certainty that the people inside were *not* going to buy! This "sales" approach is certainly negative visualization at it worst (or best—I'm not sure which!) and is sadly typical of many people who choose to foresee a negative outcome for no credible reason. Positively seeing a desirable outcome in every situation is not always going to assure the perfect ending, but I can tell you that it makes a positive difference the vast majority of the time. As Zig Ziglar says, "Positive thinking won't let you do just anything—but it will sure let you do everything better than negative thinking will!" Well said, Zig!

Wright

Do you find that having a clearly defined image of the outcome is the only thing that people must do to be assured success in their life?

Carter

Identifying the target is a crucial first step, but there is more to it than simply visualizing the goal. In the second chapter of the book of James, the Bible tells us that "faith without works is dead." Belief, combined with actively living the Christian life is what James calls for. In terms of our success, we must take action (work) toward achieving the goal in addition to having the goal clearly visualized (faith) in our mind's eye.

In the world of selling for example, action means getting up off your backside and doing the work necessary to be successful. Things like prospecting for new business, cold-calling, qualifying prospects, setting appointments, composing and perfecting an effective sales presentation, rehearsing viable answers to the inevitable customer objections that may arise, making follow-up calls, and asking for referrals are all actions that must be taken and work that must be done in order to be successful in sales.

So, yes, faith without works is dead. A visualized goal without work is seldom fully achieved.

Wright

In addition to a very busy speaking and training schedule you also do consulting work within the fire protection industry. Do you find that most of the organizations you consult with and the individuals you work with one-on-one in those companies are operating without clearly defined goals?

Carter

I am not sure that it is accurate to say that "most" of the organizations I consult with are operating without goals, David, but I have found that most of the ones struggling are often the ones lacking goals. I have seen some companies in which the concept of having goals (including quotas or expectations for their people) is completely foreign to them. As soon as measurable and achievable goals are established for the organization as a whole and for the people who work there, things do start changing for the better.

In one company I was working with, I was disappointed to learn that virtually no one in the sales department had been given any sort of a sales quota or production target for the year. As a result, none of the salespeople had a clue as to whether they were performing well or failing. Management provided no usable feedback to them. There existed a visible lack of motivation and purpose that you could see on faces and hear in voices. A mood of complacency permeated throughout the entire company. No one in the sales department was performing well, but no one knew it because they were never told what "performing well" meant. It was a sad waste of talented people's abilities and efforts.

The organizations that are alive and successful are so by design. Management has set measurable and achievable goals for the entire team and for each individual member. Each salesperson is crystal clear as to what he or she must achieve for the year, the month, the week, and in some cases, the day! The atmosphere is charged. People are excited and enthusiastic about their jobs and the prospect of hitting their targets and are motivated by the hope of reaping the rewards associated with the achievement. A sales organization without clearly defined goals is doomed to mediocrity at best—if they survive at all.

Wright

So you believe in quotas? Hasn't *quota* almost become a "bad word" in progressive sales organizations in recent years?

Carter

I am certainly not one to use foul language David, but quotas are certainly very necessary in today's sales organizations. If it is the word itself that makes people a bit uneasy, well then, they must select another one. The goal, the expectation, the target, or the magic number—all mean the same thing. Call it whatever word you are comfortable with just as long as everyone on the team has one!

In addition to having the goal or target or quota in place, people need to be held accountable to the achievement of it. Here again, the Bible teaches a valuable sales management lesson. In the Old Testament the prophet Jeremiah says that, *"The heart is deceitful above all things, and desperately wicked: who can know it?"* (Jeremiah 17:9). Now, I do not want to be negative and say that all people are dishonest, but, as the preacher said on Sunday morning, "You don't have to plant weeds in the garden! A child does not need to be taught to fib and cheat—he will do it on his or her own naturally."

Salespeople also will take a shortcut now and then. They will get a bit lazy and sloppy in their sales efforts and might cease to do the things that must be done to be successful if they are not held accountable by an attentive manager. Call reports are documents that salespeople are asked by their managers to complete on a regular basis. Call reports keep salespeople accountable for their activity. The report provides a picture of where and how that salesperson has spent his or her time, what telephone calls were made, presentations delivered, follow-up calls made, and generally what was accomplished. Reports are effective management tools. All of this activity is necessary on the part of the salesperson—in addition to that clearly defined vision for success we discussed earlier—to ensure that the quota is met and the desired goal is achieved.

Wright

Bruce, you have been working with salespeople for nearly thirty years now. What do you believe makes for a successful salesperson in this day and age?

Carter

Successful salespeople come in all sizes, shapes, colors, ethnic, religious, and social backgrounds. Some are the stereotypical, back-slapping, joke-telling, high-profile, extroverted types while others are much more subdued, introverted, and quiet. I have worked with salespeople who are very cerebral and educated and with others who have had only minimal formal education. Successful salespeople can come in a wide array of styles and models.

Although there are varied differences among them, there are a few notable similarities as well that are common to most of the real success stories. As the top half dozen qualities or characteristics of the most successful, I would list the following traits:

Honesty—You might be wondering if I am saying that one cannot be dishonest and make a sale. No, I am not saying that at all. In fact, you certainly *can* be dishonest and make a sale—there is no doubt about that—but it is unlikely you will ever build a sales career that way. Once again, that wise and timeless book states it clearly when the Apostle Paul in Galatians says, *." . . for whatsoever a man soweth, that shall he also reap"* (Galatians 6:7). I have yet to see a dishonest salesperson who built a successful sales career by cheating, lying, and taking advantage of people. Dishonesty in a marriage, home, family, or business setting will eventually lead to the fall of the institution. Dishonesty in sales will invariably have the same result—death of a sales career.

Polished Communication Skills—Good salespeople are polished speakers, not in the sense that they are skilled public speakers necessarily; but rather, that they are highly effective in their verbal interactions with people one-on-one and sparkling presenters of their company's products and services.

Good salespeople speak simply. They are careful to use only words, phrases, and terminology that customers can understand and that are not over the prospective buyer's head. People seldom make a positive purchase decision if they do not understand the details of the transaction. The problem is that the prospective buyers' pride will seldom allow them to admit to the salesperson that they do not understand the details of the product or service they are considering. Rather than saying they do not understand, they simply say, "I'll think it over and get back with you later" (i.e., "Don't call me, I'll call you"). Average to poor salespeople walk away from a sales call like that wondering why the prospect did not pick up the pen, approve the paperwork, and buy. The answer perhaps is because the buyer simply did not fully understand what it was he or she was being asked to buy!

Good salespeople also speak concisely. Many domestic corporations have downsized in recent years. As a result, remaining employees are forced to wear more hats than in the past and have more work loaded on them than ever before. Many of our prospective buyers simply do not have the time to listen to some long-winded, joke-telling salesperson going on and on about trivial aspects of his or her product or service. Sergeant Joe Friday of yesteryear's television show, *Dragnet,* fame would always say, "Just the facts ma'am, just the facts." It is that concisely stated sales message that today's top salespeople understand they must provide. I have always suggested that when it comes to making sales presentations and interacting with prospective buyers, the main thing is to keep the main thing, the main thing!

Another aspect of sales communication that is vitally important to the success of the salesperson is that of listening. In our *Fire It Up!* program, I will often select an unsuspecting member of the audience and ask, "What color is my shirt?" The person's answer is always "white." "What do cows drink?" is my next question. "Milk" comes back confidently as the answer. Milk? I don't think so. Cows drink water! Listening is an essential sales skill.

Today's very best salespeople are very skilled at asking questions. By asking questions with a purpose, salespeople are able to learn what the prospective buyer needs, what specific features he or she is looking for and can and cannot afford. Utilizing effective questioning techniques sellers are able to determine buyers' hot buttons and can smoke out potential objections that buyers may have. The prospects' answers to questions can even begin to build some positive momentum in the sales presentation leading to a positive buying decision Excellent salespeople are polished communicators. They speak simply, concisely, they ask questions with a purpose, and they listen carefully to the answers.

Professional Appearance—There is no doubt about it, success has a very distinctive "look" to it. This is most evident in the world of selling. Top producing salespeople look the part of a professional by the way they dress, their grooming, their posture, their personality, and their overall demeanor. An extensive or expensive wardrobe is not a requirement for presenting a successful image, but the conservatively dressed, tastefully groomed person with an optimistic attitude and cheery disposition will outsell the individual with a negative outlook and a disheveled appearance most of the time.

Because the majority of my seminar audiences are from a segment of the fire protection industry, I have recommended that my salespeople's appearance be on the conservative side. Fire protection products and services are a *serious* thing. People are concerned about the protection of property, possessions, and people when they consider investing in fire protection. It is a most important investment. I believe that 99 percent of the time, prospective buyers of fire protection products and services are more likely to place their trust in an individual who has the appearance of a *disciplined* individual. A more casual look may be perfectly appropriate in some sales markets, but not when it comes to life safety. A conservative, spit-and-polished look is what sells in my particular field of sales and I am sure there are hundreds of other industries where the "disciplined look" is the preferred one and the look that sells.

Organizational Skills—Selling is a numbers game. The more qualified telephone calls that are placed, presentations made, and proposals delivered, the higher the likelihood that a representative will meet the required sales quota. Since it is necessary to contact and work with large numbers of people and handle high volumes of information, it is imperative that today's sales representative be highly organized. Modern technology has proven helpful in providing some very effective organizational tools, yet it remains the ultimate responsibility of the salesperson to actually use them. Whatever gadgets, tools, or systems are found to be most effective, the top producing salespeople use them to help them be efficient and organized.

Persistence—I am delighted to report that the "better-sign-on-the-dotted-line-today-because-the-price-goes-up-tomorrow" approach to selling is nearly extinct. Now don't misunderstand, even in today's selling environment sellers still like to get a positive buying decision about their products and services in a timely manner—and preferably sooner than later. Top producing salespeople are men and women who understand there is a fine line between being persistent and being rude, and they are aware of exactly where that line is. Professional sellers would agree that they would like to culminate each sales call by receiving a check or leaving with a purchase order in hand—*today*. There are certainly situations, however, where "getting the order *today*" is simply not going to happen. In those cases, wrapping up the sales call with a clear understanding in the prospective buyer's mind *and* a clear understanding in the salesperson's mind as to *what the next step is* in the buying process, is a tremendous advantage. Both buyer and seller know what is expected and can plan accordingly for the next step in the process. Top sellers are professionally persistent.

Hard Working—It is amazing how many people quit looking for work as soon as they find a job! It is true that the heavy hitters in the world of selling somehow are able to keep their internal "fires" burning month after month and year after year. The good ones remain as excited and enthusiastic about their sales career today as they were when they started, even if they've been selling for thirty years. They continue to work diligently and work hard. The sales profession involves some of the best paying hard work and lousiest paying easy work there is. Successful sellers make a lot of sales calls. They start the day early and work late into the evening if necessary. They make a high number of telephone calls and face-to-face presentations and they follow up systematically on those sales that are pending. Top producers do the things that most "average" salespeople will overlook or simply refuse to do. Yes, top sellers work hard—very hard—at their chosen profession.

The Successful Enjoy Their Work—A number of years ago I spent the day with a gentleman who was his organization's top producing sales rep. Not only was this fellow upbeat, enthusiastic, and possessed a seemingly endless reserve of energy, his co-workers said he was like that every day! At the conclusion of our day in the sales field together I asked him his "secret" for staying so upbeat and motivated on a daily basis. After a very long pause and with an obviously concerned look on his face he agreed to share his secret only if I promised not to hold it against him or inform his superiors. Uh-oh! I thought I was about to hear that this man was some kind of a hard core substance abuser. Reluctantly, I pledged to keep his answer between the two of us. "Well, you know, all of the enthusiasm and motivation and excitement that you see—sometimes I have to fake it" he said.

"Fake it?" I replied, very surprised at his answer. "You don't really like your job?"

"Oh, I just knew you would think that—that is why I did not want to tell you" he admitted. The man went on to tell me that he actually loved his job and that it was by far the best one he had ever had. He went on to admit that although he thoroughly enjoyed going to work most days, there were some days that he did not look forward to getting out into the sales field and would much rather just pull the covers over his head and stay in bed! Like many of us he occasionally had "those days."

The man further explained that when he was young, his father many years prior had advised him to always act as if he was enjoying the job, even if he was not particularly having fun on a given day. His father always felt that people enjoy doing business much more with men and women who are enthusiastic about their work and that they prefer buying from people who appear to be genuinely "into" their profession. He went on to tell me that ever since receiving his father's advice, he made a point to literally clap his hands, take a deep breath, and put on a big smile before every sales call. He made it look like he was having a ball—even if he was having one of "those days." It was apparent that the "secret" was working and working well for this six-figure-income earner.

Wright

Bruce, that's some great stuff. As a professional speaker, do you find it particularly rewarding sharing ideas and success strategies like these with your audience, knowing that the information you provide makes a positive difference?

Carter

Yes, I really do. I find it tremendously rewarding and that, I would say, is what motivates me more than anything else. It was years ago when I came to the conclusion that many people who wear the title of "salesperson" are not performing near their potential primarily because they have never been exposed to proper sales training. David, there are a lot of salespeople out there who are floundering in their careers and may even eventually give up a potentially rewarding career in sales simply because they have never been taught the proper steps to success.

In my keynote presentations, half-day workshops, and full-day seminars I work very hard to provide not only rock-solid sales strategies and techniques that are proven to work, but I also hope to create the necessary motivation, fire, and desire within people to want to excel and succeed.

My office has received countless letters, telephone calls, and e-mails from individuals who have shared their sales success stories after having participated in our training. It is very gratifying to hear of the positive changes for the better that have taken place in these people's lives, not only in their standard of living but also in their quality of life.

Wright

There are certainly many people out there who have heard your message and whose careers and lives have been changed for the better. Who were your mentors over the years and made success possible for you?

Carter

David there have been a number of people who have made a positive difference in my life, most of them do not even know the impact they had on me. There have been a few who have shaped my career and life profoundly.

Certainly the most influential two people on my life have been my mother and dad. A fellow could not have hand-picked two people to better demonstrate the steps to living a successful life than Frank and Laveda Carter. Both have been such tremendous teachers, not by what they sat me down and formally taught me, but rather by demonstrating the principles in their own lives knowing (or at least hoping) that I might be watching from the sidelines. And I was.

My father demonstrated a patience and respect for people as no other. He was slow to anger yet so very quick to forgive and forget. My father never held a grudge. He was one of the most un-self-centered people I have ever known, rarely speaking in terms of "I." He was a very organized man—from the socks in his dresser drawer to his approach and attitude toward his job. He prioritized his time effectively. Dad was very disciplined. He tackled the tough tasks first because of their importance not because they were necessarily fun to do. Dad could tell a joke and take a joke with the best of them. I rarely heard my father criticize or complain, even up to the day he died. He lived simply, expected little, and gave much. I miss the tremendous example that he was.

My mother is eighty-five years young and was the perfect partner for my father—living, loving, and laughing with him for nearly sixty years. A more ambitious person does not exist. She was and remains a hard worker. Mom, like my father, shows concern for everyone other than herself. She is truly a giving person—not a taker. My mother taught me faith in God through her very own. I do not know of a day that my mother has not spent time in quiet conversation with God in prayer thanking Him for His generosity and asking God's guidance and protection for those dear to her. A more compassionate and caring role model for success in this life could not exist.

In the early nineties I had the pleasure and privilege of working for the world's number one motivational speaker, Zig Ziglar. As a member of the Zig

Ziglar Corporation Corporate Training Department, I learned from the very best in the business about selling, public speaking, training, marketing, motivating, managing, and the importance of developing and maintaining that positive mental attitude. Working with Mr. Ziglar was invaluable and set the course for the remainder of my career.

Along with countless others around the world, Billy Graham's simple Gospel message has had a profound impact on me. David, you asked earlier about the definition of success. In the book of Matthew, Jesus asks, *"For what is a man profited, if he shall gain the whole world and lose his own soul?"* (Matthew 16:26) I believe therein lies the very best definition of success that there is. Success means living our lives in preparation for eternity.

Wright

Well Bruce, this has been a most interesting glimpse into the success thoughts of a guy who started out on the back of a Brahma bull!

Carter

Something tells me I never should have come clean with you about the bull-riding, David.

Wright

It has been a most interesting and informative conversation, Bruce. I really do appreciate your taking the time to share your insights with me and with our readers. I learned a great deal this morning and I wish you continued success.

Carter

Thank you, David, and the same to you.

About the Author

Bruce Carter is a sales professional with over twenty-five years of "in-the-trenches" experience. Bruce shares his wealth of knowledge with thousands each year through public and in-house training seminars, conference and convention keynotes, and individual, in-the-field success coaching sessions. An active member of the National Speakers Association, Bruce addresses audiences across North America delivering a message that is down-to-earth yet powerfully hard-hitting, teaching rock-solid sales techniques, customer service skills, and strategies for career success with a brand of motivation and energy that can be described as nothing short of contagious!

Bruce Carter
55 S. Lake Avenue
Cincinnati, Ohio 45246
Phone: 513.772.3778
E-mail: nafs3@msn.com
www.nafiresales.com

Chapter Nine

An interview with . . .

David Hira

David Wright (Wright)

Today we're talking with David Hira. David is an exciting and engaging inspirational speaker and magician who combines his diverse corporate and small business experience to kick off and wrap up business conferences and meetings throughout the United States and abroad. David has performed his "magic" at such places as Caesar's Palace in Las Vegas, for President George W. Bush, and on over thirty television appearances.

In business, David opened a bicycle repair shop at the age of thirteen, created a seminar for nurses teaching "a-traumatic care" to over 12,000 nurses, created and owned a thriving restaurant in Dallas, and owned a luxury day spa. In addition, David managed the southwestern region for a $4.5 billion sales company over a twenty-year career and later became a consultant to the U.S. Customs and cargo security matters to large import and export companies. David's mix of magic, humor, and real world business lessons is his winning formula that keeps audiences from 20 to 6,000 engaged, inspired, and motivated to *do* what others say cannot be done.

David, welcome to *Conversations on Success!*

David Hira (Hira)

Thanks, David, I'm so excited to be talking with you today!

Wright

After reading about all of your business and performing experience I've got to ask—how on earth you could have done so much and still look so young.

Hira

Ha! Thanks for the compliment. I always say the secret to longevity and youthfulness is simple—just choose your grandparents. I've got great genes! But seriously, I've done so much in a short time because I'm a multi-tasker. I think I probably have a little ADD, which my wife will certainly confirm. I've also just had a real zest for life. I really want to grab everything that life has to offer while I'm on this planet. I want to do so many things, I want to learn about so many things—not just do things one thing at a time; there simply isn't enough time for that! While I was running a quarter of the country for that $4.5 billion electronics company, I was still able to open and create my restaurant, begin the course on a traumatic care for pediatric nurses and whatever else I had going. It's just been a real easy thing for me to do.

That's why it always bothers me when I hear people say to high school and college students, "What are you going to be when you grow up?" And I always think why do you have to be just *one* thing?

When students ask me, I tell them, "You can be everything!" My close friend, Raymund King, was a doctor for ten years before he was a lawyer. Before that he was an ice dancer and also a magician. He has done and "become" a lot of things in life as I have. It's a shame to restrict ourselves to "being" just one thing.

For me, doing it all, embracing all that life has to offer, has another great benefit. It allows me to be, as my friend Scott Murray likes to say, a go-*giver* and not just a go-*getter*. That makes life sweet!

Wright

You started your first business, a bicycle repair shop, when you were just thirteen years old. What did that experience teach you?

Hira

My two best friends in Junior High, Peter Hinz and Jim Howard, loved to fix bikes. On a whim we opened *Spoke and Wheel Bicycle Repair* in a rented car garage in the apartments where my family lived. The apartment manager soon asked us to move out because we were fixing around a hundred bicycles every week and the people who had their cars in the garage were starting to complain.

Along the way we decided to create what we called "the ultimate bicycle." What we decided to do—without the help of the Internet by the way—was to research and find out what were the very best individual parts that we could buy for this project. We found out what were the best rims that we could buy were and then the best spokes and the best hub—and inside the hub we bought each individual ball bearings—the best of the best of the time. From the chain to the pedals to the seat post to the frame to the cables, we bought the very best of each individual component we could get. After several months, and after spending all the money we had made along the way, we finally completed this ultimate bicycle. You can only imagine how devastated we were when we road tested it and found out that it didn't run very well at all. It was awful. That was, while I didn't know it at the time, my biggest business lesson that I ever learned. I found out that it doesn't always work to put together the "best of the best."

What it really takes to make a bunch of parts work is the *compatibility* of those parts. By simply replacing a couple of parts in our bike and replaced them with parts that worked well with each other, the machine ran smoother and faster than anything we had ever seen.

I apply the same approach to building my teams and my businesses. If I have one talent in business, it is simply that I have a really good ability to build good teams. An organization of nothing but the top dogs, the "best of the best," often leads to jealousy and in-fighting and constant battles for attention, and that is just a miserable operation. Trust me on that! I work to build organizations that are balanced with the right personalities—abilities as well as disabilities—and with people who are compatible with one another and work well with one another. Now you've got an unstoppable machine that can win any race that you put them in.

Wright

So, who was your biggest role model?

Hira

My dad, hands down. He continues to inspire me to this day. He was an incredible father growing up, and he is still an incredible dad. I remember that he came home from work every single night at six-thirty, and my sister and I would rush to meet him at the door. We'd have dinner together, we'd go play ball in the backyard, or he'd take us someplace fun. Later on in the evening we'd have our baths, he'd put us to bed, and say goodnight. I didn't find out until I was in my twenties that after he put us to bed and after we were asleep it was *then* that he went back to his office and worked very late into the night. My dad taught me a tremendous lesson of how to balance my home life and my work, which I think a lot of people fail at these days.

But best of all, my dad would let my sister and me try things that he knew we might fail in. Instead of running to our aid whenever we'd start to fall, as so many parents do these days, he'd stay in the wings and simply let us fail and let us fall—and he knew that we would learn more from our failures and our mistakes than if he just came to rescue. Bill Cosby has a great line. He said, "Dads are pals nowadays because they don't have the guts to be fathers." My dad had the guts to be a great father.

Wright

I guess we all learn from our mistakes. Would you say that mistakes are the best way to learn?

Hira

Well, I've been a great student of learning from mistakes, but I took the shortcut. My Dad had a great saying. He said, "When you grow up, if you ever have your own business or manage people, always hire one *lazy* person because they'll find the shortcuts to everything!" So I've always said, "I'm that guy!" I'm really not lazy, but I do like to find the shortcuts. It allows me to get a lot more accomplished.

Around age seventeen I decided to start surrounding myself with people far older than myself, and I mean *far* older. Most of my friends were in their fifties, sixties, and seventies. I asked them questions all the time. I wanted to learn from their mistakes. And interestingly enough, I learned more from the people society would consider failures then I did from the "successful" people. They had more lessons to share with me on what *not* to do and what they wished they had done differently. They were so open with me and willing to share what they knew.

My wife Angela thinks that one of my best traits to this day is that I know what I don't know, and I'm always quick to go to my circle of friends and advisors whenever I don't know what to do. She likes that most of my circle of friends are in that sixties, seventies, and eighties category. Times may change, but the simple principles of business, people, and life never change—they are absolute.

Wright

So you believe in having mentors or advisors. Who else was an influence in your own personal success?

Hira

I'd have to attribute my great mom for my personality and also for getting me started in performing. I was in fourth grade and I was in trouble all the time at school, not because I was mean, but because I was the class clown. And it was this unbridled kind of energy that even the teachers didn't really know how to handle. My mother was exasperated all the time because I was such a handful.

Jim Henson's Muppets were just in their infancy on television and my mother saw that I had a real interest in these Muppets of his. The mother of a friend of mine sewed and my mom got her to make my first puppet. It seemed that I suddenly had a way to channel my energy and my creativity though this puppet. I started doing puppet shows and I got the attention and laughs I was looking for.

In my twenties I got to meet Jim Henson. I didn't realize that he had been such an incredible influence on me. In the short time I had with Jim I asked him, "Can you tell me what it is about your Muppets that makes them so unique and different? They just resonant with people like no other puppet has ever done." He told me his secret. He said, "We create a new puppet, then we pick out a puppeteer who we think is compatible with that puppet. We send him off in the studio for a full week by themselves, and I charge them with a simple task: find every little thing that puppet can do." He said that at the end of the week the puppeteer would come back and show him every single thing that the puppet could do, every little nuance, every little wink or gesture or smile or whatever he could find. And then Jim said, "I would tell these puppeteers to just make the *most* out of every little thing the puppet can do, and the things it can't do will never be noticed."

I got to thinking, was he talking to me about puppets? Or was he talking to me about *me*, and you, and all of us? Because that is the truth, we always concentrate on what we can't do, what our disabilities are. You might say that you don't have a degree, that you don't have time, that you're getting a divorce or that your kids are in trouble—a bunch of reasons why you don't reach your goals and dreams. And through these Muppets Jim Henson really taught me one of the greatest lessons of all: make the most of every little ability that you *do* have and you'll stun everyone around you and stun yourself as well!

Wright

Show business has been a part of your career all of your life. Why did you decide to become a magician?

Hira

I remember telling my dad, "Dad, when I grow up I want to be a magician." Want to know what he said? He said, "You can't do *both!*"

When I started as a puppeteer I found myself trapped behind the puppet theater, and I wanted to be out in *front*. That winter my dad took me to the car show in Chicago, which is where I grew up, and I got to see my first live magician performing at one of the car exhibits. I was instantly hooked on magic and knew this would get me out in front of the puppet theater.

I began performing magic shows to every kind of venue all through junior high and high school. It was in high school that the world was changing. Inflation had taken over, people were standing in long lines for gas, people were running on fear, and many of my teachers in high school were pushing their negative views and fears on us students in the classroom.

In particular I had a teacher named Mr. Gollan who was both my economics teacher and my driving instructor. Every single day he would tell us that our generation would never own a house. He would tell us over and over what we would never be, what we couldn't have, and what we would never achieve. He constantly told us all the things that weren't going to happen for us. I don't know if he was using reverse psychology, but I was sick of his "stinkin' thinkin'."

I realized that through my simple magic shows I had the ability to show people that anything was possible! I had the ability to show people that anything can be done; I could inspire people to find ways to do things instead of reasons why they couldn't. After all, as a magician I get to *do* what other people say can't be done—so now I get to show people that they have the same power in their lives as I do as a magician. I get to show people that they can achieve anything and have the power to make their dreams come true. We may not be able to do everything, but we can do *any* thing. It's all about focus, desire, persistence, and passion.

Wright

You say that nothing is impossible. Many managers report that it is nearly impossible to motivate people in the workplace. How have you been able to motivate people to get things done for you?

Hira

I've worked in almost every kind of industry, I've owned a number of businesses, worked hundreds of other businesses, and I've worked with almost every kind of employee from high-tech sales people to clerical and administrators to CEOs to warehouse assembly workers, and I know that whatever the skill level or whatever the educational level of these people might be, these things have always been true:

1. You can't motivate people to do anything they don't want to do. It doesn't mean you can't get them to do it, it just means that you can't *motivate* them to do things that they don't want to do.
2. Everyone is motivated. It's true of every person on the planet.
3. To get things done you have to realize that people are motivated to do things for *their* reasons and not for your reasons.

Knowing this, I start every presentation I give with this one question, "Why are you working for this company?" I tell my audiences that I work because I love my family and I want them to live in a great home and a safe neighborhood. I want my family to have access to great sporting events and the arts and shopping, and I want them to be able to travel. I want my wife and kids to be able to experience all the cool things that God has made available for us on this planet. And for me to make all of this happen, it just happens to take a boatload of money! So that's why I *get* to jump out of bed each morning and take on the day.

As Zig Ziglar said so perfectly, "You can get everything in life you want if you'll just help enough other people get what *they* want." So for me to achieve my goals—and we'll talk about my business goals in particular—I have to find out what motivates each of my employees. It's simple to say to a bunch of sales guys that we have to meet this month's quota and sell ninety-eight cars on this lot by the end of this month. But why should they care? There's nothing in it for *them*. So instead, I have to find out what's in it for them—what is it that each of them are trying to achieve for their lives. And once I can identify and relate to each individual's personal goals I will know what motivates him or her, and I know what actions and programs I need to set up to help these people achieve their goals, which in turn will help me achieve my business goals.

Wright

Your internal and external customers from your restaurant, day spa, and corporate industries have all said that you are the king when it comes to "customer service." What is the secret to providing great customer service?

Hira

Well it's nice that you've heard that! The simple rule of customer service, of course, is to do unto others as you would have them do unto you. That's really the bottom line. But how do we train our employees and our teams of people to achieve this in real terms?

What I've done is I've narrowed it down to six principles on how to get employees to first care for and respect themselves, then respect others, and then they are able to deliver great service. These principles may seem shocking to you in the context of customer service. They are simple principles that my parents and my grandparents taught me, but they have an enormous impact on an organization. So here are the six principles that I believe in for an organization to have world class employees who will deliver world class service:

1. Look sharp.
2. Look everyone in the eye and smile.
3. Be the first to speak and the last to speak.
4. Know your stuff.
5. Make things right.
6. Keep your word.

In my presentations I expound on each of these and I ask managers to teach each of these principles, one a week, for six weeks, and then repeat them, and repeat them, and repeat them until people are actually *trained* to do them. If everyone learns to do these things customer service is a natural outcome. Once these principles are taught and implemented, many of the companies I've taught this to report that they actually experience a lasting change in the culture of their business. They actually see a change in how their people interact with each other.

Self-respect, mutual respect, and the desire to serve one another is the result. Sales increase, customer retention increases, and employee turnover decreases. Pretty cool, huh?

Wright

Wow. I can see the possibilities! People say you are an inspiring and fun presenter. What makes your presentations so different?

Hira

I genuinely love people. Because of my combination of being an entertainer first, plus having the experience from all of my mentors and of my own firsthand experiences from so many industries, the combination is very unique. Some speakers have such a vast knowledge, but sometimes they have an inability to deliver that information in an entertaining way or in a way that gets people to *care*. Then there are some speakers who are incredibly entertaining, but it's evident that they don't have the real life business experience and don't have any credibility with their audience. I'm "the missing link"! Many of my clients tell me that, judging from their post conference surveys, I've been the highest rated speaker they've ever had. I'm thrilled when they tell me that their people ask for me to come back time and time again. It means that their people really cared about our time together.

Wright

Do you have any last thoughts for our readers?

Hira

You bet. I'd like to ask those who are reading this, "*How do you want to be remembered?*" What do you want people to say about you when you leave the office or convention or even the family reunion? What will people say about you? Sometimes when I ask people they hang their heads in shame when they think of the things that they've done or the way that they might have treated others and I like to reassure them that there's still time to fix things. Listen to this: "No one can make a brand new start my friend, but anyone can start from *here* and make a brand new end!" The moment you decide to better yourself, the world becomes a better place. Its as true for me as it is for you. Let's make our time here *count*.

Wright

Our readers are going to get a lot out of this chapter, and I really appreciate the time you've taken to talk with me.

Hira

Thank you for allowing me to share my experiences with others. Life is good!

About the Author

David's mix of magic, humor, and real-life business experience is his winning formula for keeping people engaged, inspired, and motivated to *do* what others say is impossible. David is available internationally to transform events from the ordinary to the extraordinary!

"One of life's greatest joys is doing what others say cannot be done!"

David Hira
E-mail: david@davidhira.com
Phone: 469-688-3954
www.davidhira.com

Chapter Ten

An interview with . . .

Daved Beck

David Wright (Wright)

Daved Beck is the founder of *Evolution The Next Level*. The conception of the *ETNL* began as a way for Daved to express himself through creativity. He has been teaching, choreographing, directing, producing, and coaching in the arts for over twenty years.

Daved co-creates with several companies in the United States.

In 2004 he began the next level of his life and dream by going back to school, something he wanted to do and thought he would never be able to accomplish, and he succeeded. He moved through fear and received his coaching certification through The Fearless Living Institute founded by Rhonda Britten.

Daved, welcome to *Conversations on Success*.

Daved Beck (Beck)

Thank you so much for having me; it is an honor to be here.

Wright

Daved, I know you've heard many definitions of success, but how do *you* define success?

Beck

First, I want to thank you for this opportunity for me to embrace and to be living in this very moment—this moment that is one of my dreams and visions for my life. It feels so amazing and fulfilling to acknowledge this moment and to acknowledge myself for showing up and saying, "Yes, this is what I want."

For me to show up in opportunities that present themselves to say, "Yes" to the co-creation of my successful life is my definition for success. It is "the present moment," being all of who I am in this present moment. Success is yes, I did it, I showed up and I connected and I danced in the moment.

Wright

Who and what determines success?

Beck

The only person who can really determine my success is me—my heart and my mind. What determines my success is how I show up in the gift of life. The gifts are the opportunities that life has to offer me.

I am so grateful to live in a world that I can, be, do, and say whatever I choose and live in a world where anything is possible. If I can imagine, if I can visualize, then I can create. I can create what I imagine.

What also determines success for me is how I acknowledge the steps and the goals that I create and how I move in those steps in what I envision for my life. It doesn't matter how big or how small a step is. What matters is how am *I* showing up and how am *I* creating my life? How am *I* arranging the "yesses" of my life?

Wright

How and when do you know when you are successful?

Beck

I know when I'm successful when I'm showing up for my life in passion. Being in my passion is what being a cocreator is and is all about. To be in passion and to co-create is about love—being passionate/loving of what I'm creating, loving in the present moment, loving the "co" of the creation, and loving me.

When I create the visions of my life, when I take the steps toward my imagination and what my imagination says is possible, then I am successful.

Wright

You've used the phrase "Showing Up." Do you mean showing up as opposed to procrastination or just simply not being involved?

Beck

Yes it is both. Procrastination, not being involved—not showing up—is really about fear. Life can pass me by if I'm just sitting on the couch in front of the television set; however, I choose to dance, I choose to dance in this world, and I choose to connect with all the people of the world. Showing up is investing in my life and what I want for my life.

Wright

Aside from personal role models, who are the people who have served as your role models for success?

Beck

I consider someone a role model when I'm inspired. When I'm inspired it then becomes personal. I'm inspired by confidence, truth, and unconditional love. Someone who is willing to fully self-express and be the truth of who he or she is becomes an inspirational leader in my life.

I have hundreds and even thousands of inspirational leaders in my life. Some of those leaders I want to acknowledge are in physical form, and some I have not met as of yet (and I say "as of yet" because someday I will). Among the people I would like to meet are: Madonna, Janet Jackson, Wayne Dyer, and Ester and Jerry Hicks. I also have inspirational leaders who are not in physical form such as: Martin Luther King, Jesus, Alvin Ailey, and Bob Fossie.

There are so many others. I acknowledge others with whom I've connected in my life. Many are personal friends of mine, my dance students, my grandmother, and even other people with whom I've come into casual contact; even people walking across the street can be inspirational leaders for me. Maybe they are walking with their shoulders back with a bounce in their step and looking me in the eye. I'm inspired by that walk and maybe I'll go and create their walk in a dance.

Anybody I come into contact with can be and is a role model because each and every person is inspirational.

Wright

What do you think are the biggest obstacles people face in trying to become successful?

Beck

There are so many obstacles and really it all comes down to one. Some of the obstacles are the judgments that we place on ourselves. I'm not good enough, he or she is better than I am. We start comparing ourselves with one another. When we start comparing we are not seeing and embracing the gift we are and the gift we have to give.

We try to be perfect when there really is no "perfect." Actually everything is perfect and it is perfect the way it is.

We don't have time. I don't have time to go there. Time is ours and time is what we make of it.

Another obstacle is "I can't"—I can't do that, I can't see that, I don't know how. The truth is that we can do anything we want. We can say anything we want. Are we willing to speak the truth? Are we willing to take that risk and show ourselves that we can?

I just named a few obstacles, but really the bottom line is "fear." Fear is the biggest obstacle we have in trying to become successful. When we recognize that we are afraid right now, then we get to choose and ask: Do I want to move through this fear right now? Do I want to actually embrace this fear and dance with fear and dance in freedom to create even more freedom and create the success I want for my life? Absolutely—I want to move through fear because I do not want to live my life in fear, I want to live in freedom.

Wright

As I understand it, dance is a highly disciplined activity. Are you highly disciplined and where does that come from?

Beck

Dance can be disciplined. When I was younger I trained forty hours a week. I went to a performing arts high school and on top of that I was also going to three other dance studios simultaneously.

The way I view discipline is investment. Am I loving what I am doing and giving my all? Am I disciplined? Absolutely! Am I in dance class forty hours a week now? *No!* Do I teach my classes—am I disciplined in my choreography in my dance classes? Yes, because I am creating. I love what I'm doing. When I'm in my passion it's really not discipline it's love—love in what I am doing and love in what I am creating. I'm so grateful to be doing what I love to do.

Wright

What drives you to be successful?

Beck

The opportunities and the possibilities that life has to offer me. And being able to master my fears. When the fear comes up that says, "I can't do that" or "I don't know how," I know it's fear because I can do anything I imagine. I can be anyone I want to be. What drives me is evolving to the next level of my life and succeeding in what I want to accomplish, and following my heart in following my dreams and vision for my life.

Wright

The difference between some of the great teachers I've known, as opposed to some of the lesser, in my opinion, is the investment they give to their students. What I mean by "investment" is the investment of time, energy, and love beyond caring. Does that enter into your success pattern?

Beck

Absolutely, it goes back to showing up. If I'm not showing up, then I'm not investing. If I'm not saying, "Yes, I want this and here I am" or "I want this" and not show up, then I'm not investing. Fear will then have me by its grip and then I'm comparing myself, judging myself, and the excuses that can get in my way can include: I don't have time, I don't know how. That is all fear. It is when I'm willing to recognize that I'm afraid and fear is present when I get more passionate because I know I will get through this—it is just fear.

Wright

You spoke about evolution, what evolves you to the next level of success in your life?

Beck

There are nine gifts that I want to share with you that evolve as I evolve.

1. **Energy**—Where is my energy focused and what energy am I putting out there? Is my energy empowering or disempowering? By "energy" I mean where and how am I passionate?

2. **Visualization**—Imagination—What do I want to do, what do I want to create, where do I want to go? I ask myself and my clients these questions. I practice visualizing—seeing myself in what I want and what I want to create for my life.

3. **Optimizing**—What works for me what doesn't work for me? What has worked for me before and doesn't work for me now? What are my priorities? What are my commitments? Who and what am I committed to and what kind of support system do I have? Is it optimizing my support team around me? Who can support me in getting me to where I want to go?

4. **Love**—What do I love to do? How do I love myself? How am I nurturing and taking care of myself so I can show up in love.

5. **Utilizing Tools**—What tools have I learned to use through my life that support me? What are the proactive, successful ways that will support me in being in freedom? Am I utilizing everything I've learned throughout my life? This goes back to number three, Optimizing. Am I utilizing everything that has worked for me—utilizing the love that is all around me and offered to me?

6. **Time**—Time is one of the biggest excuses that I hear from my clients and an excuse I used to use. I often said that I didn't have *time* to do that! What it goes back to is what are my priorities and what are my commitments? Am I committed to myself or am I committed to another? We must use discipline in order to create. We must be willing to put ourselves first and commit to what we want for our life.

7. **Intensions**—What do I intend? What do I want? What do I want to feel? What do I want to create? How do I want to show up in this world and how do I want to show up in my life? Am I willing to walk the talk? Am I willing to stand in integrity?

8. **Be Open**—I must be open to the new ways of accomplishing my goals and be open to express how I feel. I must be open to change. There are so many times that I might think that I don't have the "right" answer and yet everything is right. Maybe it is just a new way

of doing something, a new way of saying something, a new way of dancing. I must definitely be open to the gifts that the world has to offer me. When we intend, we will receive.

9. **Newness**—What have I felt, said, or done that I've never done or said before? What is new in my life? I must acknowledge that newness in my life and acknowledge that newness that I get to create moving forward.

These gifts are what evolve me to the next level of my life and my success.

Wright

If you could give one gift to the world what would that be and what could that do?

Beck

We already have all the gifts that we need in co-creating the success that we desire. What I really want for the individuals of the world is to be aware and acknowledge their own personal creativity and their own personal power in their life.

When we become aware of what we are creating in our lives then we no longer remain a victim to life. When we unconditionally love what we are creating that means we are unconditionally loving ourselves.

I guess it is creating unconditional love. Unconditional love has no judgments and unconditional love has no blame. Unconditional love doesn't segregate. Unconditional love doesn't try to be perfect because everything is perfect. We are perfect now; he or she is perfect as they are. Unconditional love doesn't settle. Unconditional love dances with fear and moves through fear in freedom to love anyone and anything.

Wright

If you could choose one way to shift the world to living in absolute freedom what would you do?

Beck

The way that I'm shifting the world for freedom is already taking place. I am so excited about it because I am living one of my dreams. I'm showing up and being in this present moment, accepting and embracing the opportunity to share the gift I am. So it is me knowing that I'm a gift and sharing the gifts that I have. I'm doing it now, I am shifting the world into more freedom right now because I am moving through my own personal fears and creating freedom.

Wright

Is that nurturing oneself, accepting oneself or understanding oneself or a combination of all the above?

Beck

It is a combination of all of the above. It is saying, "Yes, I'm here. I have a purpose in this world. I'm a gift. I was brought into this world by my parents, I was given the gift of life, and I have something to offer."

It is accepting who I am. It's knowing who I am. It's believing in who I am and what I create because I create the freedom of my life. No one else can create freedom for me, only I can do that.

I can support others in creating freedom for themselves. Others can support me in creating freedom for me; however, I'm the only one who gets to choose what I am going to do.

Wright

A great man once told me that if I am walking down the road and find a turtle on top of a fence post I can bet that he did not get there by himself.

Beck

Absolutely, I want to quote one of the inspirational leaders in my life, Rhonda Britten: "No one can be fearless alone!" We all need support. That is why the world is full of people; we create the world. There are millions, billions, trillions of people in this world and if we would all work together and unconditionally love and create that unconditional love, then we could have everything we want.

Wright

What is the message you want people to hear so they can learn from your success?

Beck

The message I want the readers to know is that you can *be, do,* and *have* whatever you want. Embrace the gift of life. Embrace the gifts that life has to offer you. Acknowledge the gift that you are and the gifts that you have to offer. Say "Yes" to you. Say *"Yes,* this is what I want" and *"Yes* I want to create my life, *"Yes* I want to live," and *"Yes* I want to live in freedom."

It just takes willingness and accountability in saying "Yes" to you—to speak the truth of your desires and to acknowledge each and every step that you take in creating the freedom of your own mind.

Wright

What a great conversation. I really appreciate all this time you've taken with me today to answer all these questions. I hope I haven't put too much pressure on you. I have learned a lot from your answers.

Beck

Thank you so much. This was such a pleasure and honor. Thank you for supporting me in fulfilling one of my dreams and fulfilling the success in my life.

About the Author

Daved Beck is the founder of Evolution—The Next Level. The conception of Evolution—The Next Level (ETNL) began as a way for Daved to express himself though creativity. He has been teaching, choreographing, directing, producing, and coaching in the arts for over twenty years.

He is a national choreographer, dance instructor, director, producer, author, and has co-created some of his life successes with such companies as GI Alliance Dance Company, 5 Star Boogie Productions, The Fearless Living Institute, Summers Academy of Dance, and many more.

In 2004 he began the next level of his life and dream by going back to school, something he wanted to do and thought he would never be able to accomplish, and he succeeded. He moved through fear and received his coaching certification through The Fearless Living Institute founded by Rhonda Britten.

ETNL has evolved into coaching individuals, couples, and groups to create the life of success they want and desire by moving through and shifting the emotional fears that stop people from creating and living a life of inspirational success.

Life is a dance and with Daved's utilization and integration of fearless living, dance training, coaching skills, corporate, and life experience, his clients get the opportunity to partner with their soul, moving through fear and dancing in freedom, while gaining tools and building their skills in a life of absolute success.

Daved Beck
Evolution—The Next Level
Phone: 312-307-1929
E-mail: Daved@evolutionthenextlevel.com
www.evolutionthenextlevel.com

Chapter Eleven

An interview with . . .

Danny Cox

David Wright (Wright)

Today we're talking with Danny Cox, professional speaker and author. Danny spent ten years flying supersonic all-weather fighters in the United States Air Force. In addition to this he was a test pilot and air show pilot as well as a speaker to civilian organizations in surrounding cities that were hard hit by sonic booms. He was internationally known as *The Sonic Boom Salesman*.

Upon leaving the Air Force he joined one of the nation's largest sales companies. A year later he was promoted to sales manager and guided his office in its industry-leading, record-breaking pace of doubling, tripling, and quadrupling old records. Four years after joining that corporation he was promoted to First Vice President and assigned a district of eight offices and a staff of over one hundred and forty people. By teaching the same sound leadership principles to the eight branch managers that he had used, the company saw old records shattered. As morale and productivity soared, the percentage of employee turnover dropped to near zero. In a five-year period, production increased over 800 percent.

Due to the increasing demands for innovative leadership and teamwork techniques that work, Danny packed his bags and has hardly unpacked them since. He is in great demand by companies and organizations nationally and internationally.

Highly acclaimed platform skills have earned Danny a place in the National Speaker Association Speaker Hall of Fame, a designation for platform excellence awarded to less than 3 percent of the over 3,200-member National Speakers Association. Danny is also an elected member of the elite Speakers Roundtable, a group of twenty of the most popular speakers in North America.

Now, Danny is one of America's busiest speakers and author of several books, including *Leadership When the Heat's On, Seize the Day: 7 Steps to Achieving the Extraordinary in an Ordinary World,* and *There Are No Limits: Breaking the Barriers in Personal High Performance.*

Danny, welcome to *Conversations on Success.*

Danny Cox (Cox)

It's my pleasure, David!

Wright

You are defined by some as an "accelerationist." I have never heard that term applied to a professional speaker before. Will you explain what it means?

Cox

It means faster movement, higher efficiency, increased productivity, boldly crossing barriers, and an adventurer at high speed. I came up with that because I didn't want to bill myself as a motivational speaker. The term "motivational speaker" has become a term that's almost overused. Yes, my audiences wide up motivated, but I thing "accelerationist" is better. The other reason is that I just spent ten years flying supersonic fighters at almost twice the speed of sound, so that fits in with my resume!

Wright

As a boy I used to go out to Tyson-McGee Airport in Knoxville, Tennessee, to watch those F86s take off!

Cox

I love the F-86. That was the first airplane I flew that would go supersonic. It was an F86D and I was flying in Valdosta, Georgia, at Moody Air Force Base. The only way you'd get that supersonic speed was to climb to 43,000 feet, push the throttle all the way up, wipe the afterburners, and roll upside down into a vertical dive; then you could get through the sound barrier. I'll tell you, it was a real thrill watching the Okefenokee Swamp approach your windshield at supersonic speed!

Wright

So actually the pilot had to make it supersonic, right?

Cox

Yes, that's right!

Wright

So how did you go from flying fighters to the business world to speaking?

Cox

After ten years flying supersonic fighters I had an interview with the Thunderbirds, the Air Force Aerobatic Team. I was told, "Congratulations, you made it!" The only problem was that I was in the Air Defense Command, the all-weather group, they were in D Fighter Command. My command said, "No, we need all-weather pilots and you can't go."

That knocked me out of flying with the team so I thought I'd shape up the Air Force. I sent in my resignation thinking that would really do the trick on them, and they accepted it. I was a civilian overnight and trying to figure out what I was going to do the rest of my life.

A good friend of mine, Hal Needham the stuntman, said, "Get out here to southern California. If I can make it out here as a tree trimmer from St. Louis surely you, the son of a coal miner from Marion, Illinois, would be able to handle it."

So I headed out to the West Coast to fly with the airlines. They loved me as long as I was talking to them on the phone. They said, "Twenty-four of those high-performance, fighter timed test pilots and air show pilots have never had an accident. We're going to mail you an application today."

"Now, wait a minute," I said. "Before you do, what are your height requirements?"

"Five feet eight," came the reply.

"That's my goal—to be five feet eight!"

And they wouldn't hire me.

Looking back on it now, it was the best thing that ever happened to me. I'd been called The Sonic Boom Salesman in the Air Force because it had been my job to not only knock off way more than my share of plaster and brick and knock out way more than my share of windows, but after that I had to go out and explain to upset and hostile civilian audiences why these sonic booms were "good" for them, which is a tough sale I might add!

So I joined the sales company and I sold for a year. Then the company said I was selling enough to be a manager of one of their offices. "Starting when?" I asked.

They said, "This afternoon."

So it didn't take me very long to be a leader of people. They put me through their entire management training program while I was standing there, which is a common problem in a lot of corporations—here, you're a manager, congratulations.

I went out to this little office and so-called "managed" this office for a year. The company came to me one more time and said, "Now then, we want you to take over the top office of our thirty-six offices!"

I couldn't wait to get back to that office, because that's where I had been a brand new salesperson the first year out of the Air Force. You can't imagine how those top people remembered me as a brand new guy and now they had to welcome me back as the boss! They hated me with a passion. I kept saying to them, "Don't think of me as the boss, just think of me as a friend who's always right!" My goal was to turn them into copies of me, and *surprise*—they didn't want that! What a missed opportunity for them.

We went from number one to thirty-six of thirty-six offices in three months' time, and I knew I was in trouble. My boss came out to see me and said, "I made a mistake by making you a manager; I'm looking for your replacement." I told him I was going to have to have time to learn how to do this.

"You don't have much time," he said.

So I went to work on *me* instead of them, which I found was the real secret. I learned a lot of things. We built back up to number one. Then we plateaued out at number one. This fascinated me—why did we get back up to where we once were and then not keep going? I realized that we were up against a self-imposed barrier. When you total up everybody's self-imposed barriers you've got the office's self-imposed barrier.

I brought each one of my people in and said, "I don't want you to worry about breaking anybody else's sales record. I just want you to worry about breaking your own on a daily, weekly, monthly, quarterly basis." I'd really give them a pep talk when they got close to their own record. Once they saw their old record starting to fall, the energy went sky high and we broke office records and company records and industry records!

Then they gave me a district to manage. That was eight offices and a hundred and forty some odd people. Over a five-year period we achieved an 800 percent increase in production!

I knew I was onto something then. I knew I could go out and teach what I'd learned, so I hit the road as a speaker and, as they say, "the rest is history"! I've been doing it with all kinds of organizations, even Air Force squadrons have hired me, so it's been a varied career. I've never been bored.

Wright

Your bestselling book, *Leadership When the Heat's On,* is endorsed by John Maxwell, the *New York Times* bestselling author and famous speaker. What makes this book different from most books on leadership?

Cox

That book went through twelve printings in its first edition, and it is in its second edition. I think the secret is that I kept copious notes of everything I tried while I was managing the office, and later on in the sales district. I kept track of what worked and what didn't work. I passed that on to the managers who were working for me. I laid out the book in the same way that I would talk and teach all the things every manager should know. As I've said before, when my boss was looking for my replacement, I had to pay $10,000 per copy of my book! All those things I did became my life preserver. I learned from all kinds of industries.

When my boss said he was looking for my replacement I thought, "Where do I go and what do I do?"

Well, it struck me that when I was in a fighter squadron and somebody had a real hairy life-threatening emergency, but they got it safely on the ground, we always said, "Congratulations, you lived through it!" What I did was to go a little deeper. I would buttonhole the pilot and say, "Let's go to the Officer's Club, I want to talk with you." I wanted to find out everything that went wrong and what they tried. It wasn't enough to know that the pilot had made it back—I wanted to know how.

I did the same thing in the business world. I knew that when my boss was looking for my replacement, I was going to have to learn and learn *fast*. I started calling people I'd read stories about in the business sections of magazines and newspapers. They weren't in my industry, but the people-principles are basically the same. That's when I started learning. And what I learned is in my book!

Wright

The table of contents of *Leadership When the Heat's On* reads like a reference book on how to solve problems and guide employees. Is that what you intended?

Cox

Actually, I wanted it to be my own experiences or those of my managers who worked for me—those I worked with and who had tried something we eventually proved worked. These experiences were what I wanted to put into the book. I wanted it to be a real hands-on book—everything from how to recruit to how to pick a new manager to how to handle a prima donna—those kinds of things. As a result, the book's just loaded with those kinds of practical things.

Wright

If you had to pick two or three characteristics that make up a great leader, what would they be?

Cox

First of all, a person is not born with these characteristics I talk about. These are characteristics you have to develop. I learned that from all my mentors.

I would say the first and foremost is uncompromising integrity. That's got to be the steel-reinforced foundation for all the rest of the characteristics you develop. This means that you have to keep your customers not just in focus, but in crystal clear focus—there's a difference. If you just have them in focus it's too easy to get sidetracked in the lesser things that are going on in the company or the industry or the world, and then you've lost sight of the customer who is so important to you. We've seen a lot of that happen with business leaders who have all the other good characteristics, but didn't have crystal clear focus and they don't last long. To get the best results great leaders need to give good customer service with crystal-clear focus. I've told managers that their first line of customers are the people who work for them. Employees treat customers the same way they are treated by management, which sometimes keeps managers awake for a few nights, it's true.

Some companies that I've worked with have been sidetracked from giving good customer service. They looked at it as though it was a *fad*, thinking, "We don't have to serve customers like we used to." However, if you tell that to your customers, they'll land on you hard!

Uncompromising integrity keeps you focused on your customers, but also it keeps you from getting sidetracked into lesser things and the "petty" things that go on in organizations. Pettiness is the biggest drain on energy that you can have in an organization.

The other thing is the great leaders I've studied were excellent at working their priorities—not just setting priorities, but working their priorities. If you work your priorities, it gives you a feeling of stability under pressure. If you can be stable under pressure you can also be a great problem-solver.

If you want to be a great problem-solver, work it backward. You've got to develop stability under pressure, and you do it by working your priority list. Too often the biggest problem is we don't start with number one, we start with number five. Why? Well, number one through four are *hard*, but those are the priorities you've got to work on!

Back in the Ozark hill country where I grew up we put it this way, "If you got a frog to swallow, don't look at it too long. And if you got more than one to swallow, swallow the biggest one first!" And that's become a catch phrase and my signature story. I get letters from people who write, "You made me a frog-swallower!" The interesting thing about working on things by priority I learned from one of my mentors. When the great leaders get done with number one on their priority list they *don't* go to number two—they go to the new number one! And when they get done with that they don't go to number three, but they go to the new number one, and so on down the list. Even the last thing on the list for the day is done right.

The third one is enthusiasm.

All great leaders have enthusiasm! I asked one of my mentors once, "How do you get that in-depth enthusiasm that's contagious for the people around you? Not that phony kind of stuff where you jump up and down and scream a lot." He said that you get that kind of enthusiasm by witnessing the accomplishment of your daily goals—not just your tasks, which are part of a larger plan—then you can't help but be enthusiastic.

Wright

Since June of 1969 when I opened my first business, my business philosophy has always been, "As the people grow, so grows the organization." I stole that from a guy down in Texas, Paul Meyer. Your book, *Seize the Day: 7 Steps to Achieving the Extraordinary in an Ordinary World*, seems to embrace this philosophy.

By sharing your wisdom through success stories, have you found that people who have read your book are changing for the better?

Cox

Oh yes! It's really interesting, especially now that my books are in twenty-six different languages. I get e-mails from all over the world commenting on my books. That book has really been a great seller!

I got one e-mail from a young golf pro who said that he had listened to my audiotape. He had cancer and was going toward being a full-time pro on tour. He said he listened to that tape at least two hundred times while he was going through chemo therapy—he didn't go on the tour, but he's one of the instructors on the PGA faculty. He has given me far more than my share of credit for that the ideas in there.

Seize the Day is what I taught my salespeople when they plateaued out. The steps in the book show you how to change a plateau and move on to the next higher level of productivity. Using the system I put in the book was how we kept getting better and better.

Wright

In *Seize the Day* you take cues from great achievers such as George Bernard Shaw and Thomas Edison. Who have been important people in your life who have helped make you the person you are?

Cox

I mentioned Hal Nedham a while ago; he's called "the King of the Stuntmen." He's a friend of mine; our friendship goes all the way back to my Air Force fighter pilot days. He had a big affect on me by talking me into coming out to California. He's the one who wrote and directed *Smokey and the Bandit* and *Cannonball Run*. He's had fifty-six major bone breaks. I asked him if he ever worried about getting killed, and he said, "Danny, if I get killed tomorrow, I'm going to know that what I did with my life was exactly what I wanted to do! How many people do you know who can say that?"

"Not many," I said. And that became a big thing for me too—I want to make sure that I'm doing exactly what I want to do with my life!

The other one is Mike Vance. He was a close associate of Walt Disney. He and Diane Deacon wrote *Think Out of the Box, Break Out of the Box*, and the third book was called *Raise the Bar*. I heard him speak the week after my boss said he was looking for my replacement.

The most important and interesting person who had an affect on me was Jim Newton. He wrote a book called *Uncommon Friends*. When he was twenty years old back in the 1920s he started running around with Henry Ford, Harvey Firestone, Thomas Edison, Charles Lindberg, and Dr. Lexus Courell, a Nobel Prize winner who invented microsurgery and co-invented the first heart valve with Charles Lindberg as well as the artificial heart.

Charles Lindberg was the only one who was close to Jim in age, he was three years older than Jim—but I met Jim when he brought me down to speak to his company in Fort Myers, Florida. When I met him he was seventy-seven. He had started this real estate company when he was sixty-six, and he and his wife were trying to live on social security. They'd put away money at one time but they'd lived longer than they'd thought they were going to, prices had gone up, and he had started on a shoestring. He couldn't even afford a regular real estate office; he'd rented a portion of a glassed-in porch there at one of the hotels. He said he just had room for one desk and he couldn't afford a phone so he opted for advertising. People would get in touch with them with the pay phone on the wall of the hotel.

When I met him eleven years later he had fifteen real estate offices and he was seventy-seven years old. His wife was six years older than he was—she was eighty-three! They had almost two hundred salespeople working for them, and they were the number one company in Fort Myers, Florida.

He became like a father to me. My wife and I spent a lot of time down in Fort Myers taking to Jim and Ellie Newton. We were really like family. Jim was with us up until 1999. He never use the term "died," he would always say "graduated." We were sitting there having lunch with his wife and him and another friend of ours, Anne Lindberg, Charles' widow. We were talking about the lasting impact that these men had on the world today. And I asked, "What did those great men have in common? Did they have anything in common?" Jim said, "Yes, they had three driving forces: a sense of purpose, a spirit of adventure, and a desire for continued personal growth."

I said, "Good gosh, you could build a book around those things!" The book, *There are No Limits: Breaking the Barriers in Personal Performance*, is what it's all about. I said, "You could build a company around those things, you could build a family around those things—purpose, adventure, growth! So Jim had a major effect on me.

And then Dr. Robert H. Schuller, who started The Crystal Cathedral, has been a friend for a long time. As he always says, "Tough times don't last, tough people do!" He's had a big effect too.

So those are some of the people who have helped me along the way.

Wright

I've interviewed Dr. Schuller before; he's a real man—a great guy!

Cox

Yep!

Wright

Problems, obstacles, challenges—no matter what they are called—are difficult for many people in business as well as personal life. Your book, *There Are No Limits*, seems to be written for those who are in a rut or even those who have failed before. What do you tell these people?

Cox

Often it's not so much a "rut" as it is a plateau. My definition of a self-imposed barrier is this: a self-imposed barrier is not a wall around your life—it's simply the margin of your life where you haven't written anything yet. We look at the dividing line that runs between our developed potential and our undeveloped potential. We look at that line as though it's a wall. In the book I discuss that and how important it is to break through that barrier. You do it with purpose, adventure, and growth.

I use the illustration from my flying days. Every time I crawled into a new fighter plane, nothing looked the same, nothing was in the same place. Maybe it was two hundred, maybe four hundred miles an hour faster than anything I had ever flown before. I'd think I'd hit the Peter Principle—this is one I'm probably not going to be able to handle.

You get out there to the end of the runway and you line up and you look down that long, long runway and you think, "Well, this is going to be interesting." As we always said back home, "If you ain't got a choice, be brave!" Pull the trigger and ride the bullet. I lit those afterburners of the F101-B (never fly the "A" model of anything, a little bit of philosophy there), I went full blast off the runway. An hour later I'm thinking, "This is a piece of cake!"

When we look at new things that same way, we wonder, "Am I going to be able to handle this? Am I going to be able to try?" Hey, push the throttle all the way up! Go for it! You've probably noticed that I use a lot of my flying analogies in my talks and my books.

Wright

How important is it to keep growing and what are the benefits?

Cox

One of my clients on the East Coast has great quotes up on the wall at his corporate headquarters in one inch brass letters. I guess the company meant for them to stay. They went through quite a turnaround a few years ago. They were an old line company. As I was walking down the hallway with one of the vice presidents and reading these great quotes, there was one that really brought me to a halt. This should be on every manager's wall and it should be on every salesperson's wall. Here's what it said: "There is no saturation to education."

Isn't that a great thought?

Wright

It sure is!

Cox

And to me that's what keeps you alive. I went to a lot of survival schools in the Air Force—very interesting. A lot of my flying was done in single engine fighters—so if you lose your engine, how many do you have going? None! I went to every survival school I could find because I wanted to make sure that if I ever had to open the door and "leave the building" I wanted to hit the ground and be able to live until somebody found me.

Every class I went to at survival school always had some tough old sergeant who would really get you all fired up in the classroom first, and then he would say, "Tell you what is going to happen to you, Lieutenant; tell you what is going to happen to you, Colonel," and he'd go through all the different ranks. "Now then, someday you're going to have that airplane come apart and someday you're going to eject. You're going to come down just fine, and when we finally find you maybe two or three days later you're going to be *dead*—graveyard dead." I thought that whatever he says next I'm going to write down. He said, "Unless you have a feeling of accomplishment on a daily basis, your morale will kill you quicker than anything else!"

I realized that the same thing applies to the business world.

I defy anybody to go in on Monday and do Monday, then on Tuesday do Monday again and on Wednesday do Monday one more time, on Thursday do Monday one more time, on Friday do one more repeat of Monday, and then try to have a fabulous weekend! You can't do it. You haven't felt like you've accomplished anything. So that's the morale problem you can get yourself into by not continuing to grow and develop.

I asked Jim Newton once, "Give me an example of how these famous friends of yours looked at continuing education." He said that he was with Mr. Edison one time when they had a news conference and one of the newspaper reporters asked Mr. Edison, "When are you going to retire, Mr. Edison?"

Mr. Edison always had that twinkle in his eye. He looked at the reporter and said, "The day before my funeral."

I thought that was a good attitude! And he almost made it, by the way. I think it was six days from his last day—he was in the lab until the day he "graduated."

Wright

Finally, has your ten years of flying experience had a profound effect on your writing and professional speaking, and if so, how?

Cox

Okay. Well, I've learned a lot from my test flying days. I didn't do test flying like Chuck Yeager; I didn't do the prototype testing—mine was in the squadrons. If something was wrong with an airplane and the mechanics couldn't find out what the problem was, I'd take the airplane up and try to get the airplane to do it again, which made for some exciting experiments, to say the least! Then once they said they had it fixed, then I would take it up again and see if they *really had* fixed it. So I think that's like good leadership too, sometimes you just have to go in after the problem whatever it might be!

Wright

It's a life-saving technique too, isn't it?

Cox

Oh, yes it is. I did a lot of high-speed testing. You can always do more than you think, you know?

I was doing testing in Arizona and I flew this big F101-B Voodoo, which was seventy feet long, twenty-two and a half tons, and a 1,200-mile-per-hour airplane. I put it down on the deck at twenty-five feet and 700 miles per hour just under the speed of sound so they could follow me on the radar and see if there were any holes in their radar net. We always kept in mind that the sky is not the limit, the ground is! We always said that you can only "tie" the record for flying low—and that's true.

So I decided to try something new here with my business. Hey, if I mess it up at least I'm not going to get killed! That was the thing about my previous job as a supersonic fighter pilot—it was a very "unforgiving" business. You only got one mistake. That was it. I use those illustrations all the time. People relate to them, they tie in with my accelerationist title. My company is called Acceleration Unlimited.

And one other thing, this Voodoo fighter plane that I had had a bad pitch-up problem because the horizontal tail was about fifteen feet higher than the wing, so the hard pull-up shifted the fuel to the back of the airplane. The air that was coming over the wing was coming down on the tail, and it would literally tumble out of the sky! The response from the Air Force was, "Don't worry; we've built systems in to prevent that from happening." Well, I learned early that when the Air Force said "don't worry" you *should* worry!

I was going up after a U2, and he was above 60,000 feet. I was at 56,000 feet pulling nose up when the system in my airplane failed and I went into this violent tumble and lost 30,000 feet of altitude in the tumble. Fortunately I was at 56,000 when I started. I tumbled knowing that this was the ninth pitch-up the Air Force had had since they bought the airplane, and only three guys ahead of me had survived it. What saved my life, they said, was that I quit fighting the controls. I neutralized the controls and I reached up to the instrument panel. I pulled the drag chute handle that we normally used on landings when we touched down at 200 miles per hour. When I pulled the drag chute out I went from 1,200 miles per hour to zero and I was just tumbling toward a spot on the ground. I had no forward motion at all. When the drag chute came out I felt it take hold and what it did was that it got the air flowing over the wings again.

That experience corresponds to the one I had when my boss said, "I'm looking for your replacement." I had to neutralize the controls, pop the drag chute, and get away from the office for a couple of days to figure out how I was going to put everything all back together again. So I recommend that highly: neutralize the controls regularly and pop the drag chute!

Wright

What an interesting conversation, I'm not surprised that you're one of the greatest speakers in the world today. It's always a pleasure to talk with you. Very, very interesting! You have a bottom line way of putting things. The next time I fire someone, instead of saying, "You're fired," I'm going to say, "I'm looking for your replacement."

Cox

Trust me, it all means the same, right?

Wright

Oh yes!

Today we have been talking with Danny Cox who is a professional speaker and author. Highly acclaimed platform skills have earned Danny a place in the National Speakers Association Speakers Hall of Fame, a designation for excellence awarded to less than 3 percent of the over 3,000 members in the Association. He's also an elected member of the Elite Speakers Round Table. All of these men in the Round Table are great, great speakers. There's a group of twenty of them who are the most popular speakers in North America, and I have found out today why Danny is one of them.

Danny, thank you so much for being with us today on *Conversations on Success!*

About the Author

Danny Cox is an "accelerationist", or one who causes faster movement, higher efficiency and increased productivity.

He spent ten years flying supersonic all-weather fighters in the United States Air Force. In addition to this he was a test pilot and air show pilot as well as a speaker to civilian organizations in surrounding cities that were hard hit by sonic booms. He was internationally known as The Sonic Boom Salesman.

Upon leaving the Air Force he joined one of the nation's largest sales companies. A year later, he was promoted to sales manager and guided his office in its industry-leading, record-breaking pace of doubling, tripling and quadrupling old records. Four years after joining that corporation he was promoted to First Vice President and assigned a district of eight offices and a staff of over 140. By teaching the same sound leadership principles to the eight branch managers that he had used, the company saw old records shattered. As morale and productivity soared, percentage of employee turnover dropped to near zero. In a five year period production increased over 800 percent.

Due to the increasing demands for innovative leadership and teamwork techniques that work, Danny packed his bags and has hardly unpacked them since. He is in great demand by companies and organizations nationally and internationally.

Highly acclaimed platform skills have earned Danny a place in the National Speaker Association Speaker Hall of Fame, a designation for platform excellence awarded to less than three per cent of the over 3200 member National Speakers Association. Danny is also an elected member of the elite Speakers Roundtable, a group of twenty of the most popular speakers in North America.

Now, one of America's busiest speakers and author of several books, including *Leadership When the Heat's On, Seize The Day: 7 Steps to Achieving the*

Extraordinary in an Ordinary World and *There Are No Limits: Breaking The Barriers In Personal High Performance.*

Danny Cox
Acceleration Unlimited
www.DannyCox.com